Seeing the Unseen

Seeing the Unseen

Responses to Fitz-James O'Brien's 'What Was It? A Mystery'

Mathew D. Staunton, Kristine Hoyt Jouanne,
Rethabile Masilo, Cécile Chartier, Alexandra Tauvry
Agnès Fourtané & Feargus Gwynplaine McIntyre

Published in Oxford by The Onslaught Press
11 Ridley Road, OX4 2QJ
January, 2014

ISBN-13 978-0-9927238-0-4

Typeset in Le Monde Livre & Le Monde Sans,
designed, & edited by Mathew D. Staunton

Printed by LightningSource.

Contents

This book is dedicated to invisible people the world over.

And to our friend Feargus.

Mathew D. Staunton also dedicates his contribution to all children who have suffered at the hands of those who should have been protecting them; to Brice and János, their friends in Rue Erasme, the homeless people in Rue d'Ulm, and everywhere else; and to his daughter Aoife.

Kristine Hoyt Jouanne: I would like to dedicate this book to my parents, Dale and Linda Hoyt, who opened up the world for me, and to my daughter Chloé, who is its shining light. I also dedicate it to all those who are still struggling to bring the "invisible" members of our societies out where we can see them and appreciate them for their full value. I also thank Mathew Staunton for involving me in this project, which has been so fulfilling.

Agnès Fourtané: To my dear niece ane nephew, Louisa and Gustave.

Rethabile Masilo: I dedicate this work, and the feelings it may produce in you, to my children, Thabo and Lineo

Alexandra Tauvry: To my brother Maxime

This project was born at the bottom of Rue Mouffetard while I was having a coffee with my colleague Cécile Chartier. I was looking for a subject that would appeal to a wide range of academics, writers, artists, and designers, and around which I could build an exhibition and a conference. Cécile suggested Fitz-James O'Brien's wonderful but very much neglected tale 'What Was It? A Mystery' and I was convinced within minutes. What better vehicle to bring such a disparate group of people together than a mysterious account of the horrific death of an invisible being? As an example of 19th-century science fiction or horror, 'What Was It?' is an important and seductive text. But when you consider it as a critique of the society in which it was written and realize that this critique functions just as well when mapped onto any society, it starts to read like a masterpiece.

Cécile joined me in the organization of the conference and we soon discovered that O'Brien's tale was as appealing as we had hoped. Researchers in Irish, European, and American literature were keen to deconstruct the text, question the role and reliability of the narrator, and explore all of the potential meanings of the invisible ghoul. Historians saw all sorts of maligned groups and communities in the perceptual blind spot inhabited by the nameless, voiceless creature. Artists and designers wanted to experiment with photography, video, sculpture, UV-sensitive ink, blind embossing techniques, and projecting film onto constantly moving surfaces to trick our eyes, make the invisible visible, and disturb us by revealing things we didn't really want to see in the first place. It quickly became clear that the notions of social and historical invisibility would be recurring themes in both the conference and the exhibition.

This book reflects the content of the conference only. Many of the pieces included in the exhibition were interactive and ephemeral and cannot be reduced to a simple photograph in a book. I would, nonetheless, like to thank Laura Acquaviva, Liberty Adrien, Delphine Breissand, Steven Briand, Anais Caura, Hugo Deverchère, Margot Duroux, Laure Fissore, Benoit Julienne, Smail Kanouté, Jade le Kim, Morgan le Pechon, Tristan Maillet, Julia Manset, Marc Maoine, Pierre Mazingarbe, Victor Melchy, Flore Mounier, and Yonah Riollet for their contributions. Julia, Benoit, and Victor deserve special thanks for designing and building the exhibition.

I would also like to thank everyone who made both the conference and the exhibition possible. As my own school refused to provide any material, logistical, financial, or moral support for the project (but claimed responsibility for it afterwards) I was obliged to look elsewhere for venues and funding. This turned out to be a very good thing for us as we made new and lasting friends in the institutions in our neighbourhood.

Sheila Pratschke and her team at the Centre Culturel

Irlandais welcomed us with open arms and provided us with an excellent space for our exhibition. They also very generously promoted the event at their own expense. More precious still was the constant presence during the preparation of the exhibition of the Centre's technical manager Philippe Saltel. Philippe contributed more than his fair share of time and energy to the project, and stayed with us through the night and into the early hours of the morning before the opening to make sure that everything was ready. Thanks Philippe, Sheila, and everyone at the CCI.

Our thanks also go to François Michaud, Director of the Bibliothèque Sainte-Barbe who let us use a beautifully restored amphitheatre in the newly refurbished library (on the site of the 15th century Collège de Sainte-Barbe) for our conference. There are few venues in Paris that would have suited us more and we were made to feel very welcome in this wonderful historical monument.

Professor Wesley Hutchinson, head of Pôle Irlande at Université Paris 3—Sorbonne Nouvelle and president of the SOFEIR, deserves a very special thank you. Without his support, encouragement, and trust we could not have achieved even a fraction of what we did. The funding he secured for us from PRISMES allowed us to transform the exhibition space at the CCI into a platform for multiple visual interpretations of O'Brien's tale and share the different visions of the artists and designers mentioned above with the visitors to the Centre.

The essays and poetry included in this book were all read during the conference. Some texts, my own included, have evolved over the four years since they were first originally presented and appear today in revised form. Rethabile Masilo's poems are included with the generous permission of the poet, our friend and a good friend to this project. Feargus Gwynplaine MacIntyre's essay is included with his permission, given shortly before he took his own life in June 2010. His paper was read *in absentia* by Ret during the conference and is reproduced here as it was given to us, with minor changes to punctuation. I have also included one of the illustrations from his 1994 novel *The Woman Between the Worlds* which were projected during the conference.

A crucial part of our project, but not one that could be fully enjoyed in the context of a conference, was the new French translation of 'What Was It? A Mystery' realised by Agnès Fourtané. I am delighted to include the text of her 'Qu'était-ce? Un Mystère' in this book, which would be very much incomplete without it.

Thank you to everyone who attended the conference and visited the exhibition.

And thank you Kristine, Agnès, Alexandra, Ret, and Cécile for contributing to this book and proofing the text.

Dr Mathew D. Staunton,
Oxford, January 2014.

All endnote references to the text of 'What Was It? A Mystery' correspond to the version of the tale included in this volume, pp. 1-21.

What Was It?

A Mystery

Fitz-James O'Brien

It is, I confess, with considerable diffidence that I approach the strange narrative which I am about to relate. The events which I purpose detailing are of so extraordinary and unheard-of a character that I am quite prepared to meet with an unusual amount of incredulity and scorn. I accept all such beforehand. I have, I trust, the literary courage to face unbelief. I have, after mature consideration, resolved to narrate, in as simple and straightforward a manner as I can compass, some facts that passed under my observation in the month of July last, and which, in the annals of the mysteries of physical science, are wholly unparalleled.

I live at No.— Twenty-sixth Street, in this city. The house is in some respects a curious one. It has enjoyed for the last two years the reputation of being haunted. It is a large and stately residence, surrounded by what was once a garden, but which is now only a green inclosure used for bleaching clothes. The dry basin of what has been a fountain, and a few fruit trees, ragged and unpruned, indicate that this spot, in past days, was a pleasant, shady retreat, filled with fruits and flowers and the sweet murmur of waters.

The house is very spacious. A hall of noble size leads to a vast spiral staircase winding through its center, while the various apartments are of imposing dimensions. It was built some fifteen or twenty years since by Mr. A——, the well-known New York merchant, who five years ago threw the commercial world into convulsions by a stupendous bank fraud. Mr. A——, as every one knows, escaped to Europe, and died not long after of a broken heart. Almost immediately after the news of his decease reached this country, and was verified, the report spread in Twenty-sixth Street that No.— was haunted. Legal measures had dispossessed the widow of its former owner, and it was inhabited merely by a caretaker and his wife, placed there by the house agent into whose hands it had passed for purposes of renting or sale. These people declared that they were troubled with unnatural noises. Doors were opened without any visible agency. The remnants of furniture scattered through the various rooms were, during the night, piled one upon the other by unknown hands. Invisible feet passed up and down the stairs in broad daylight, accompanied by the rustle of unseen silk dresses, and the gliding of viewless hands along the massive balusters. The caretaker and his wife declared that they would live there no longer. The house agent laughed, dismissed them, and put others in their place. The noises and supernatural manifestations continued. The neighborhood caught up the story, and the house remained untenanted for three years. Several persons negotiated for it; but somehow, always before the bargain was closed, they heard the unpleasant rumors, and declined to treat any further.

It was in this state of things that my landlady—who at that time kept a boarding-house in Bleecker Street, and who wished to move farther up town—conceived the bold idea of renting No.— Twenty-sixth Street. Happening to have in her house rather a plucky and philosophical set of boarders, she laid down her scheme before us, stating candidly everything she had heard respecting the ghostly qualities of the establishment to which she wished to remove us. With the exception of two timid persons—a sea captain and a returned Californian, who immediately gave notice that they would leave—all of Mrs Moffat's guests declared that they would accompany her in her chivalric incursion into the abode of spirits.

Our removal was effected in the month of May, and we were all charmed with our new residence. The portion of Twenty-sixth Street where our house is situated—between Seventh and Eighth Avenues is one of the pleasantest localities in New York. The gardens back of the houses, running down nearly to the Hudson, form, in the summer time, a perfect avenue of verdure. The air is pure and invigorating, sweeping, as it does, straight across the river from the Weehawken heights, and even the ragged garden which surrounded the house on two sides, although displaying on washing days rather too much clothesline, still gave us a piece of greensward to look at, and a cool retreat in the summer evenings, where we smoked our cigars in the dusk, and watched the fireflies flashing their dark-lanterns in the long grass.

Of course we had no sooner established ourselves at No.— than we began to expect the ghosts. We absolutely awaited their advent with eagerness. Our dinner conversation was supernatural. One of the boarders, who had purchased Mrs. Crowe's *Night Side of Nature* for his own private delectation, was regarded as a public enemy by the entire household for not having bought twenty copies. The man led a life of supreme wretchedness while he was reading this volume. A system of espionage was established, of which he was the victim. If he incautiously laid the book down for an instant and left the room, it was immediately seized and read aloud in secret places to a select few. I found myself a person of immense importance, it having leaked out that I was tolerably well versed in the history of supernaturalism, and had once written a story, entitled 'The Pot of Tulips,' for *Harper's Monthly*, the foundation of which was a ghost. If a table or a wainscot panel happened to warp when we were assembled in the large drawing room, there was an instant silence, and every one was prepared for an immediate clanking of chains and a spectral form.

After a month of psychological excitement, it was with the utmost dissatisfaction that we were forced to acknowledge that nothing in the remotest degree approaching the supernatural had manifested itself. Once the black butler asseverated that his candle had been blown out by some invisible agency while he was undressing himself for the night; but as I had more than once discovered this colored gentleman in a condition when one candle must have appeared to him like two, I thought it possible that, by going a step farther in his potations, he might have reversed his phenomenon, and seen no candle at all where he ought to have beheld one.

Things were in this state when an accident took place so awful and inexplicable in its character that my reason fairly reels at the bare memory of the occurrence. It was the tenth of July. After dinner was over I repaired, with my friend Dr Hammond, to the garden to smoke my evening pipe. Independent of certain mental sympathies which existed between the Doctor and myself, we were linked together by a vice. We both smoked opium. We knew each other's secret, and respected it. We enjoyed together that wonderful expansion of thought, that marvelous intensifying of the perceptive faculties, that boundless feeling of existence when we seem to have points of contact with the whole universe—in short, that unimaginable spiritual bliss, which I would not surrender for a throne, and which I hope you, reader, will never—never taste.

Those hours of opium happiness which the Doctor and I spent together in secret were regulated with a scientific accuracy. We did not blindly smoke the drug of paradise, and leave our dreams to chance. While smoking, we carefully steered our conversation through the brightest and calmest channels of thought. We talked of the East, and endeavored to recall the magical panorama of its glowing scenery. We criticized the most sensuous poets—those who painted life ruddy with health, brimming with passion, happy in the possession of youth and strength and beauty. If we talked of Shakespeare's *Tempest*, we lingered over Ariel, and avoided Caliban. Like the Guebers, we turned our faces to the East, and saw only the sunny side of the world.

This skillful coloring of our train of thought produced in our subsequent visions a corresponding tone. The splendors of Arabian fairyland dyed our dreams. We paced the narrow strip of grass with the tread and port of kings. The song of the rana arborea, while he clung to the bark of the ragged plum tree, sounded like the strains of divine musicians. Houses, walls, and streets melted like rain clouds, and vistas of unimaginable glory stretched away before us. It was a rapturous companionship. We enjoyed the vast delight more perfectly because, even in our most ecstatic moments, we were conscious of each other's presence. Our pleasures, while individual, were still twin, vibrating and moving in musical accord.

On the evening in question, the tenth of July, the Doctor and myself drifted into an unusually metaphysical mood. We lit our large meerschaums, filled with fine Turkish tobacco, in the core of which burned a little black nut of opium, that, like the nut in the fairy tale, held within its narrow limits wonders beyond the reach of kings; we paced to and fro, conversing. A strange perversity dominated the currents of our thought. They would not flow through the sun-lit channels into which we strove to divert them. For some unaccountable reason, they constantly diverged into dark and lonesome beds, where a continual gloom brooded. It was in vain that, after our old fashion, we flung ourselves on the shores of the East, and talked of its gay bazaars, of the splendors of the time of Haroun, of harems and golden palaces. Black afreets continually arose from the depths of our talk, and expanded, like the one the fisherman released from the copper vessel, until they blotted everything bright from our vision. Insensibly, we yielded to the occult force that swayed us, and indulged in gloomy speculation. We had talked some time upon the proneness of the human mind to mysticism, and the almost universal love of the terrible, when Hammond suddenly said to me. "What do you consider to be the greatest element of terror?"

The question, I own, puzzled me. That many things were terrible, I knew. Stumbling over a corpse in the dark; beholding, as I once did, a woman floating down a deep and rapid river, with wildly lifted arms, and awful, upturned face, uttering, as she sank, shrieks that rent one's heart, while we, the spectators, stood frozen at a window which overhung the river at a height of sixty feet, unable to make the slightest effort to save her, but dumbly watching her last supreme agony and her disappearance. A shattered wreck, with no life visible, encountered floating listlessly on the ocean, is a terrible object, for it suggests a huge terror, the proportions of which are veiled. But it now struck me for the first time that there must be one great and ruling embodiment of fear, a King of Terrors to which all others must succumb. What might it be? To what train of circumstances would it owe its existence?

"I confess, Hammond," I replied to my friend, "I never considered the subject before. That there must be one Something more terrible than any other thing, I feel. I cannot attempt, however, even the most vague definition."

"I am somewhat like you, Harry," he answered. "I feel my capacity to experience a terror greater than anything yet conceived by the human mind—something combining in fearful and unnatural amalgamation hitherto supposed incompatible elements. The calling of the voices in Brockden Brown's novel of *Wieland* is awful; so is the picture of the Dweller of the Threshold, in Bulwer's *Zanoni*; "but," he added, shaking his head gloomily, "there is something more horrible still than these."

"Look here, Hammond," I rejoined, "let us drop this kind of talk, for Heaven's sake! We shall suffer for it, depend on it."

"I don't know what's the matter with me tonight," he replied, "but my brain is running upon all sorts of weird and awful thoughts. I feel as if I could write a story like Hoffman tonight, if I were only master of a literary style."

"Well, if we are going to be Hoffmanesque in our talk, I'm off to bed. Opium and nightmares should never be brought together. How sultry it is! Good night, Hammond."

"Good night, Harry. Pleasant dreams to you."

"To you, gloomy wretch, afreets, ghouls, and enchanters."

We parted, and each sought his respective chamber. I undressed quickly and got into bed, taking with me, according to my usual custom, a book, over which I generally read myself to sleep. I opened the volume as soon as I had laid my head upon the pillow, and instantly flung it to the other side of the room. It was Goudon's *History of Monsters*—a curious French work, which I had lately imported from Paris, but which, in the state of mind I had then reached, was anything but an agreeable companion. I resolved to go to sleep at once; so, turning down my gas until nothing but a little blue point of light glimmered on the top of the tube, I composed myself to rest.

The room was in total darkness. The atom of gas that still remained lighted did not illuminate a distance of three inches round the burner. I desperately drew my arm across my eyes, as if to shut out even the darkness, and tried to think of nothing. It was in vain. The confounded themes touched on by Hammond in the garden kept obtruding themselves on my brain. I battled against them. I erected ramparts of would-be blankness of intellect to keep them out. They still crowded upon me. While I was lying still as a corpse, hoping that by a perfect physical inaction I should hasten mental repose, an awful incident occurred. A Something dropped, as it seemed, from the ceiling, plumb upon my chest, and the next instant I felt two bony hands encircling my throat, endeavoring to choke me.

I am no coward, and am possessed of considerable physical strength. The suddenness of the attack, instead of stunning me, strung every nerve to its highest tension. My body acted from instinct, before my brain had time to realize the terrors of my position. In an instant I wound two muscular arms around the creature, and squeezed it, with all the strength of despair, against my chest. In a few seconds the bony hands that had fastened on my throat loosened their hold, and I was free to breathe once more. Then commenced a struggle of awful intensity. Immersed in the most profound darkness, totally ignorant of the nature of the Thing by which I was so suddenly attacked, finding my grasp slipping every moment, by reason, it seemed to me, of the entire nakedness of my assailant, bitten with sharp teeth in the shoulder, neck, and chest, having every moment to protect my throat against a pair of sinewy, agile hands, which my utmost efforts could not confine—these were a combination of circumstances to combat which required all the strength and skill and courage that I possessed.

At last, after a silent, deadly, exhausting struggle, I got my assailant under by a series of incredible efforts of strength. Once pinned, with my knee on what I made out to be its chest, I knew that I was victor. I rested for a moment to breathe. I heard the creature beneath me panting in the darkness, and felt the violent throbbing of a heart. It was apparently as exhausted as I was; that was one comfort. At this moment I remembered that I usually placed under my pillow, before going to bed, a large yellow silk pocket handkerchief, for use during the night. I felt for it instantly; it was there. In a few seconds more I had, after a fashion, pinioned the creature's arms.

I now felt tolerably secure. There was nothing more to be done but to turn on the gas, and, having first seen what my midnight assailant was like, arouse the household. I will confess to being actuated by a certain pride in not giving the alarm before; I wished to make the capture alone and unaided.

Never losing my hold for an instant, I slipped from the bed to the floor, dragging my captive with me. I had but a few steps to make to reach the gas-burner; these I made with the greatest caution, holding the creature in a grip like a vice. At last I got within arm's length of the tiny speck of blue light which told me where the gas burner lay. Quick as lightning I released my grasp with one hand and let on the full flood of light. Then I turned to look at my captive.

I cannot even attempt to give any definition of my sensations the instant after I turned on the gas. I suppose I must have shrieked with terror, for in less than a minute afterward my room was crowded with the inmates of the house. I shudder now as I think of that awful moment. I saw nothing! Yes; I had one arm firmly clasped round a breathing, panting, corporeal shape, my other hand gripped with all its strength a throat as warm, and apparently fleshly, as my own; and yet, with this living substance in my grasp, with its body pressed against my own, and all in the bright glare of a large jet of gas, I absolutely beheld nothing! Not even an outline—a vapor!

I do not, even at this hour, realize the situation in which I found myself. I cannot recall the astounding incident thoroughly. Imagination in vain tries to compass the awful paradox.

It breathed. I felt its warm breath upon my cheek. It struggled fiercely. It had hands. They clutched me. Its skin was smooth, like my own. There it lay, pressed close up against me, solid as stone—and yet utterly invisible!

I wonder that I did not faint or go mad on the instant. Some wonderful instinct must have sustained me; for, absolutely, in place of loosening my hold on the terrible Enigma, I seemed to gain an additional strength in my moment of horror, and tightened my grasp with such wonderful force that I felt the creature shivering with agony.

Just then Hammond entered my room at the head of the household. As soon as he beheld my face—which, I suppose, must have been an awful sight to look at—he hastened forward, crying, "Great heaven, Harry! what has happened?"

"Hammond! Hammond!" I cried, "come here. Oh! this is awful! I have been attacked in bed by something or other, which I have hold of; but I can't see it—I can't see it!"

Hammond, doubtless struck by the unfeigned horror expressed in my countenance, made one or two steps forward with an anxious yet puzzled expression. A very audible titter burst from the remainder of my visitors. This suppressed laughter made me furious. To laugh at a human being in my position! It was the worst species of cruelty. Now, I can understand why the appearance of a man struggling violently, as it would seem, with an airy nothing, and calling for assistance against a vision, should have appeared ludicrous. Then, so great was my rage against the mocking crowd that had I the power I would have stricken them dead where they stood.

"Hammond! Hammond!" I cried again, despairingly, "for God's sake come to me. I can hold the—the Thing but a short while longer. It is overpowering me. Help me! Help me!"

"Harry," whispered Hammond, approaching me, "you have been smoking too much opium."

"I swear to you, Hammond, that this is no vision," I answered, in the same low tone. "Don't you see how it shakes my whole frame with its struggles? If you don't believe me, convince yourself. Feel it,—touch it."

Hammond advanced and laid his hand on the spot I indicated. A wild cry of horror burst from him. He had felt it!

In a moment he had discovered somewhere in my room a long piece of cord, and was the next instant winding it and knotting it about the body of the unseen being that I clasped in my arms.

"Harry," he said, in a hoarse, agitated voice, for, though he preserved his presence of mind, he was deeply moved, "Harry, it's all safe now. You may let go, old fellow, if you're tired. The Thing can't move."

I was utterly exhausted, and I gladly loosed my hold. Hammond stood holding the ends of the cord that bound the Invisible, twisted round his hand, while before him, self-supporting as it were, he beheld a rope laced and interlaced, and stretching tightly round a vacant space. I never saw a man look so thoroughly stricken with awe. Nevertheless his face expressed all the courage and determination which I knew him to possess. His lips, although white, were set firmly, and one could perceive at a glance that, although stricken with fear, he was not daunted.

The confusion that ensued among the guests of the house who were witnesses of this extraordinary scene between Hammond and myself—who beheld the pantomime of binding this struggling Something—who beheld me almost sinking from physical exhaustion when my task of jailer was over—the confusion and terror that took possession of the bystanders, when they saw all this, was beyond description. The weaker ones fled from the apartment. The few who remained clustered near the door, and could not be induced to approach Hammond and his Charge. Still incredulity broke out through their terror. They had not the courage to satisfy themselves, and yet they doubted. It was in vain that I begged of some of the men to come near and convince themselves by touch of the existence in that room of a living being which was invisible. They were incredulous, but did not dare to undeceive themselves. How could a solid, living, breathing body be invisible, they asked. My reply was this. I gave a sign to Hammond, and both of us—conquering our fearful repugnance to touch the invisible creature—lifted it from the ground, manacled as it was, and took it to my bed. Its weight was about that of a boy of fourteen.

"Now, my friends," I said, as Hammond and myself held the creature suspended over the bed, "I can give you self-evident proof that here is a solid, ponderable body which, nevertheless, you cannot see. Be good enough to watch the surface of the bed attentively."

I was astonished at my own courage in treating this strange event so calmly; but I had recovered from my first terror, and felt a sort of scientific pride in the affair which dominated every other feeling.

The eyes of the bystanders were immediately fixed on my bed. At a given signal Hammond and I let the creature fall. There was the dull sound of a heavy body alighting on a soft mass. The timbers of the bed creaked. A deep impression marked itself distinctly on the pillow, and on the bed itself. The crowd who witnessed this gave a sort of low, universal cry, and rushed from the room. Hammond and I were left alone with our Mystery.

We remained silent for some time, listening to the low, irregular breathing of the creature on the bed, and watching the rustle of the bedclothes as it impotently struggled to free itself from confinement. Then Hammond spoke:"Harry, this is awful."

"Aye, awful."

"But not unaccountable."

"Not unaccountable! What do you mean? Such a thing has never occurred since the birth of the world. I know not what to think, Hammond. God grant that I am not mad, and that this is not an insane fantasy!"

"Let us reason a little, Harry. Here is a solid body which we touch, but which we cannot see. The fact is so unusual that it strikes us with terror. Is there no parallel, though, for such a phenomenon? Take a piece of pure glass. It is tangible and transparent. A certain chemical coarseness is all that prevents its being so entirely transparent as to be totally invisible. It is not theoretically impossible, mind you, to make a glass which shall not reflect a single ray of light—a glass so pure and homogeneous in its atoms that the rays from the sun shall pass through it as they do through the air, refracted but not reflected. We do not see the air, and yet we feel it."

"That's all very well, Hammond, but these are inanimate substances. Glass does not breathe, air does not breathe. This thing has a heart that palpitates—a will that moves it—lungs that play, and inspire and respire."

"You forget the strange phenomena of which we have so often heard of late," answered the Doctor, gravely. "At the meetings called 'spirit circles,' invisible hands have been thrust into the hands of those persons round the table—warm, fleshly hands that seemed to pulsate with mortal life."

"What? Do you think, then, that this thing is—"

"I don't know what it is," was the solemn reply; "but please the gods I will, with your assistance, thoroughly investigate it."

We watched together, smoking many pipes, all night long, by the bedside of the unearthly being that tossed and panted until it was apparently wearied out. Then we learned by the low, regular breathing that it slept. The next morning the house was all astir. The boarders congregated on the landing outside my room, and

Hammond and myself were lions. We had to answer a thousand questions as to the state of our extraordinary prisoner, for as yet not one person in the house except ourselves could be induced to set foot in the apartment.

The creature was awake. This was evidenced by the convulsive manner in which the bedclothes were moved in its efforts to escape. There was something truly terrible in beholding, as it were, those second-hand indications of the terrible writhings and agonized struggles for liberty which themselves were invisible.

Hammond and myself had racked our brains during the long night to discover some means by which we might realize the shape and general appearance of the Enigma. As well as we could make out by passing our hands over the creature's form, its outlines and lineaments were human. There was a mouth; a round, smooth head without hair; a nose, which, however, was little elevated above the cheeks; and its hands and feet felt like those of a boy. At first we thought of placing the being on a smooth surface and tracing its outline with chalk, as shoemakers trace the outline of the foot. This plan was given up as being of no value. Such an outline would give not the slightest idea of its conformation.

A happy thought struck me. We would take a cast of it in plaster of Paris. This would give us the solid figure, and satisfy all our wishes. But how to do it? The movements of the creature would disturb the setting of the plastic covering, and distort the mold. Another thought. Why not give it chloroform? It had respiratory organs—that was evident by its breathing. Once reduced to a state of insensibility, we could do with it what we would. Doctor X—— was sent for; and after the worthy physician had recovered from the first shock of amazement, he proceeded to administer the chloroform. In three minutes afterward we were enabled to remove the fetters from the creature's body, and a well-known modeler of this city was busily engaged in covering the invisible form with the moist clay. In five minutes more we had a mold, and before evening a rough fac-simile of the mystery. It was shaped like a man—distorted, uncouth, and horrible, but still a man. It was small, not over four feet and some inches in height, and its limbs revealed a muscular development that was unparalleled. Its face surpassed in hideousness anything I had ever seen. Gustave Doré, or Callot, or Tony Johannot, never conceived anything so horrible. There is a face in one of the latter's illustrations to *Un Voyage où il vous plaira*, which somewhat approaches the countenance of this creature, but does not equal it. It was the physiognomy of what I should have fancied a ghoul to be. It looked as if it was capable of feeding on human flesh.

Having satisfied our curiosity, and bound every one in the house to secrecy, it became a question what was to be done with our Enigma. It was impossible that we should keep such a horror in our house; it was equally impossible that such an awful being should be let loose upon the world. I confess that I would have gladly voted for the creature's destruction. But who would shoulder the responsibility? Who would undertake the execution of this horrible semblance of a human being? Day after day this question was deliberated gravely. The boarders all left the house. Mrs Moffat was in despair, and threatened Hammond and myself with all sorts of legal penalties if we did not remove the Horror. Our answer was, "We will go if you like, but we decline taking this creature with us. Remove it yourself if you please. It appeared in your house. On you the responsibility rests." To this there was, of course, no answer. Mrs Moffat could not obtain for love or money a person who would even approach the Mystery.

The most singular part of the transaction was that we were entirely ignorant of what the creature habitually fed on. Everything in the way of nutriment that we could think of was placed before it, but was never touched. It was awful to stand by, day after day, and see the clothes toss, and hear the hard breathing, and know that it was starving.

Ten, twelve days, a fortnight passed, and it still lived. The pulsations of the heart, however, were daily growing fainter, and had now nearly ceased altogether. It was evident that the creature was dying for want of sustenance. While this terrible life struggle was going on, I felt miserable. I could not sleep of nights. Horrible as the creature was, it was pitiful to think of the pangs it was suffering.

At last it died. Hammond and I found it cold and stiff one morning in the bed. The heart had ceased to beat, the lungs to inspire. We hastened to bury it in the garden. It was a strange funeral, the dropping of that viewless corpse into the damp hole. The cast of its form I gave to Dr. X——, who keeps it in his museum in Tenth Street.

As I am on the eve of a long journey from which I may not return, I have drawn up this narrative of an event the most singular that has ever come to my knowledge.

NOTE.—It was rumored that the proprietors of a well-known museum in this city had made arrangements with Dr. X—— to exhibit to the public the singular cast which Mr. Escott deposited with him. So extraordinary a history cannot fail to attract universal attention.

Qu'était-ce?
Un Mystère

a new translation by Agnès Fourtané

C'est, je le confesse, avec une méfiance considérable que j'aborde l'étrange récit que je suis sur le point de rapporter. Les évènements que je me propose de raconter en détails sont d'une nature si extraordinaire et si inédite que je suis tout à fait prêt à faire face à une quantité inhabituelle d'incrédulité et de mépris. J'accepte tout cela par avance. J'ai, j'en suis convaincu, le courage littéraire d'affronter le scepticisme. Après mûre réflexion, je me suis résolu à raconter, d'une manière aussi simple et directe qu'il me sera possible de le faire, des faits qu'il m'a été donné d'observer au cours du mois de juillet dernier et qui, dans les annales des mystères des sciences naturelles, sont absolument sans précédent.

J'habite au numéro —— de Twenty-sixth Street, dans cette ville. La maison est à certains égards un curieux spécimen. Depuis deux ans, elle a la réputation d'être hantée. C'est une grande demeure élégante, entourée de ce qui fut jadis un jardin, mais qui n'est désormais qu'un enclos de verdure utilisé pour faire sécher le linge. Le bassin asséché de ce qui fut une fontaine, et quelques arbres fruitiers, décharnés et non taillés, indiquent que ce lieu fut, par le passé, un lieu de retraite plaisant et ombragé, empli de fruits et de fleurs et du doux murmure de l'eau.

La maison est très spacieuse. Un couloir de noble taille conduit à un vaste escalier en colimaçon, tandis que les différents appartements sont de dimensions imposantes. Elle fut construite il y a quelque quinze ou vingt ans, par Mr A, le célèbre marchand new-yorkais, qui, il y a cinq ans de cela, propulsa le monde du commerce dans le marasme par une ahurissante fraude bancaire. Mr A, comme chacun sait, s'enfuit en Europe, et mourut de chagrin peu après. Presque aussitôt après que la nouvelle de son décès atteignit ce pays, et fut vérifiée, le bruit courut dans Twenty-sixth Street que le numéro —— était hanté. La veuve de son ancien propriétaire avait été dépossédée par des mesures judiciaires, et le bâtiment n'était plus occupé que par un gardien et son épouse, placés là par l'agent immobilier entre les mains duquel il était passé pour être mis à la location ou en vente. Ces gens déclarèrent qu'ils étaient dérangés par des bruits artificiels. Des portes s'ouvraient sans que personne de visible n'y touchât, les meubles restés là, éparpillés à travers les différentes pièces, étaient, durant la nuit, empilés par des mains inconnues. Des pieds invisibles montaient et descendaient les escaliers en plein jour, accompagnés du bruissement de robes de soie invisibles et du glissement de mains transparentes le long des balustres massives. Le gardien et son épouse déclarèrent qu'ils ne vivraient plus dans cette maison. L'agent immobilier se moqua d'eux, les renvoya et les fit remplacer. Les bruits et les manifestations surnaturelles continuèrent. Le voisinage eut vent de l'histoire et la maison resta inoccupée pendant trois ans. Plusieurs individus négocièrent pour l'acquérir mais, d'une façon ou d'une autre, toujours avant la conclusion de l'affaire, ils entendaient les rumeurs peu avenantes et refusaient d'aller plus loin dans les démarches.

Ce fut dans ce contexte que ma logeuse—qui à l'époque tenait une pension sur Bleecker Street et souhaitait déménager plus haut dans la ville—mit au point l'idée culottée de louer le Numéro —— de Twenty-sixth Street. Il se trouvait qu'elle logeait dans sa maison un échantillon de pensionnaires plutôt courageux et philosophes et elle nous exposa son projet en mentionnant avec franchise tout ce qu'elle avait entendu concernant les attributs fantomatiques de l'établissement vers lequel elle souhaitait nous déplacer. Exception faite de deux personnes craintives—un capitaine de navigation et un ancien émigré revenu de Californie, qui signalèrent immédiatement qu'ils partiraient—les hôtes de Mrs Moffat tous autant qu'ils étaient déclarèrent qu'ils l'accompagneraient dans son incursion chevaleresque au sein de la demeure des esprits.

Notre déménagement se déroula au mois de mai et nous fûmes tous charmés par notre nouvelle résidence. La portion de Twenty-sixth Street dans laquelle notre maison se trouve—entre Seventh et Eigth Avenues—est un des quartiers les plus agréables de New-York. Les jardins derrière les maisons, dont la pente court pratiquement jusqu'au fleuve Hudson, constituent, aux beaux jours, un coin de verdure idéal. L'air y est pur et revigorant, circulant comme il le fait directement vers le fleuve depuis les hauteurs de Weehawken, et même le jardin à l'abandon qui entourait la maison de deux côtés, bien qu'il contînt les jours de lessive un peu trop de corde à linge, nous offrait cependant un bout de verdure à regarder, et un lieu de retraite au frais les soirs d'été, où nous fumions des cigares entre chien et loup, et observions les lucioles faisant clignoter leurs lanternes sourdes dans les hautes herbes.

Bien entendu, à peine installés au numéro ——, nous commençâmes à attendre les fantômes. Nous attendions leur venue avec une excitation absolue. Au dîner, notre conversation était surnaturelle. Un des pensionnaires, qui avait acquis un exemplaire de *La Face obscure de la nature*, de Mrs Crowe pour son plaisir personnel, fut considéré comme un ennemi public par toute la maisonnée pour ne pas en avoir acheté vingt exemplaires. L'homme en question vivait un enfer lorsqu'il était plongé dans la lecture de l'ouvrage. Un système d'espionnage, dont il était la victime, fut mis en place. Si, par mégarde, il posait le livre, ne serait-ce qu'un instant, et quittait la pièce, quelqu'un s'en emparait aussitôt et le lisait à voix haute dans des endroits secrets à quelques heureux élus. Je devins une personne d'une importance immense, le bruit ayant couru que j'avais une certaine connaissance de l'histoire du surnaturel et que j'avais écrit un jour, pour le magazine *Harper's Monthly*, une histoire intitulée « Le pot de tulipes », dont le personnage principal était un fantôme. Si une table ou une cloison en lambris venait à trembler lorsque nous étions rassemblés dans le vaste salon, le silence se faisait instantanément et tout le monde s'attendait à entendre un bruit de chaînes et à voir apparaître une forme spectrale.

Après un mois d'excitation des esprits, ce fut avec la plus grande déception que nous fûmes contraints de reconnaître qu'absolument rien que l'on eut pu qualifier, ne serait-ce qu'à un degré infime, de surnaturel ne s'était manifesté. Un jour, le majordome noir affirma solennellement que quelque force invisible avait éteint sa bougie alors qu'il était en train de se déshabiller pour la nuit. Néanmoins, comme il m'était arrivé plus d'une fois de découvrir cet homme de couleur dans un état tel qu'il devait voir deux bougies là où il s'en trouvait une seule, il me parut possible qu'en allant plus loin dans ses libations, il aurait pu présenter ce phénomène de manière inverse, et ne voir aucune bougie du tout là-même où il aurait dû en distinguer une.

La situation en était à ce stade lorsqu'eut lieu un incident d'une nature si affreuse et si inexplicable que la seule évocation de cet événement me bouleverse. C'était le 10 juillet. Le dîner terminé, je me rendis, en compagnie de mon ami le docteur Hammond, dans le jardin pour fumer ma pipe du soir. Outre certaines affinités de caractère qui existaient entre le docteur et moi-même, un vice secret nous unissait. Nous fumions tous deux de l'opium. Chacun connaissait le secret de l'autre, et le respectait. Nous savourions ensemble cet extraordinaire déploiement de la pensée, cette merveilleuse intensification des facultés de perception, cette sensation illimitée d'exister quand on a le sentiment d'être en relation avec tout l'univers, bref, cet inimaginable béatitude de l'esprit, à laquelle je ne renoncerais pour rien au monde, et que j'espère que vous, lecteur, ne goûterez jamais, oh grand jamais.

Ces heures de bonheur procuré par l'opium que le docteur et moi passions ensemble en secret étaient réglées avec une précision toute scientifique. Nous ne fumions pas à l'aveuglette la drogue des Paradis artificiels, en laissant nos rêves au hasard. Lorsque nous fumions, nous orientions soigneusement notre conversation vers les pensées les plus lumineuses et les plus calmes. Nous parlions de l'Orient, et nous efforcions de nous remémorer le panorama magique de ses paysages flamboyants. Nous critiquions les poètes les plus sensuels, ceux qui dépeignaient la vie comme étant rougeoyante de santé, débordante de passion, heureuse de posséder la jeunesse, et la force et la beauté. Si nous évoquions *La Tempête* de Shakespeare, nous nous attardions sur Ariel et évitions Caliban. À l'instar des Guèbres, nous tournions nos visages vers l'Orient et ne voyions que la face ensoleillée du monde.

L'habile coloration du fil de nos pensées se retrouvait dans la tonalité des visions qui suivaient. Les splendeurs du royaume des fées d'Arabie habillaient nos rêves de couleurs. Nous parcourions cette étroite bande d'herbe avec la démarche et le port des rois. Le chant de la grenouille Rana arborea alors qu'elle s'accrochait à l'écorce du vieux prunier ressemblait aux accords d'orchestres divins. Les maisons, les murs et les rues fondaient comme des nuages de pluie, et des images d'inimaginable gloire se déployaient sous nos yeux. C'était une compagnie enivrante. Chacun de nous appréciait plus parfaitement encore ce vaste délice, car, même dans nos moments d'extase la plus profonde, nous avions toujours conscience de la présence de l'autre. Nos plaisirs, bien qu'individuels, n'en demeuraient pas moins partagés, vibrant et bougeant comme dans un mouvement musical harmonieux.

Lors de la soirée en question, le 10 juillet, le Docteur et moi-même nous trouvâmes d'une humeur inhabituellement métaphysique. Nous allumâmes nos grandes pipes en écume de mer, bourrées de tabac turc de grande qualité, au cœur duquel brûlait une petite noisette brune d'opium, qui, comme la noisette dans le conte de fées, renfermait au sein de ses étroites limites des merveilles inaccessibles aux rois ; nous fîmes des allées et venues tout en conversant. Une étrange perversité dominait le flot de nos pensées. Elles se refusaient à emprunter les voies ensoleillées vers lesquelles nous nous efforcions de les détourner. Pour des raisons que je ne puis expliquer, elles déviaient constamment vers des contrées sombres et solitaires, où couvait une morosité permanente. Ce fut en vain que, selon notre vieille habitude, nous nous projetâmes sur les rivages de l'Orient, et parlâmes de ses joyeux bazars, des splendeurs de l'époque d'Harun, des harems et des palaces dorés. De noirs *afreets* surgissaient sans cesse des profondeurs de notre discussion et grandissaient, comme celui à qui le pêcheur rendit la liberté depuis le vaisseau de cuivre, au point d'obscurcir toute chose brillante dans notre champ de vision. De façon imperceptible, nous cédions à la force occulte qui nous faisait tanguer et nous laissions aller à de sombres suppositions. Nous avions parlé pendant un certain temps du penchant de l'esprit humain pour le mysticisme et de l'amour presque universel du Terrible lorsque Hammond me dit soudain : « Quel est selon vous la composante essentielle de la terreur ? »

La question, je l'avoue, m'intrigua. Que beaucoup de choses étaient terribles, je le savais. Trébucher sur un cadavre dans l'obscurité ; regarder, comme je le fis un jour, une femme, emportée par le courant d'un fleuve rapide et profond, les bras en l'air dans un mouvement incontrôlé, le visage affreux et renversé, poussant, alors qu'elle s'enfonçait, des cris à vous déchirer le cœur, tandis que nous, spectateurs, nous tenions, debout et glacés à la fenêtre qui donnait sur la rivière, à une vingtaine de mètres de hauteur, incapables de faire quoi que ce soit pour la sauver, mais la regardant en silence vivre ses tout derniers instants puis disparaître. Une épave dévastée, sans âme qui vive, rencontrée à la dérive sur l'océan est un objet terrible car il suscite une terreur considérable, dont les proportions sont secrètes. Mais j'étais frappé pour la première fois par la pensée qu'il doit exister une incarnation majeure et dominante de la peur, une Reine des Terreurs à laquelle aucune autre ne doit résister. De quoi pouvait-il s'agir ? À quelle suite d'événements devrait-elle la vie ?

« Je le confesse, Hammond, répondis-je à mon ami, je n'ai jamais considéré le sujet auparavant. Qu'il doit exister une Chose plus terrible que toute autre, j'en ai la sensation. Je ne peux pas m'essayer, cependant, à la moindre définition, même la plus vague.

—Je suis quelque peu comme vous, Harry, répondit-il. J'ai la sensation de ma capacité à connaître une terreur plus grande que tout ce qu'a pu concevoir l'esprit humain jusqu'à présent. Quelque-chose combinant, en un amalgame effrayant et artificiel, des éléments jusqu'à présent réputés incompatibles. Les voix qui incitent le héros au meurtre dans *Wieland* de Brockden Brown sont quelque-chose d'affreux ; de même que l'image du gardien du seuil dans *Zanoni* de Bulwer-Lytton, mais, ajouta-t-il, secouant la tête de façon inquiétante, il existe quelque-chose de plus horrible encore que cela.

—Ecoutez moi, Hammond, répliquai-je, pour l'amour du ciel, laissons tomber ce genre de discussion. Nous en souffririons, soyez-en sûr.

—Je ne sais pas ce qu'il m'arrive ce soir, répondit-il, mais mon cerveau bouillonne de toutes sortes de pensées étranges et affreuses. J'ai la sensation que je pourrais écrire une histoire comme celles d'Hoffman ce soir, si seulement j'avais la maîtrise d'un style littéraire.

—Bien, si nous devons être Hoffmanesque dans notre discussion, je vais me coucher. L'opium et les cauchemars ne devraient jamais être abordés ensemble. Comme il fait lourd ! Bonne nuit, Hammond!

—Bonne nuit, Harry, faites de beaux rêves.

—Et vous, pauvre diable, rêvez d'*afreets*, de fantômes et d'enchanteurs. »

Nous nous séparâmes, et chacun chercha sa chambre respective. Je me déshabillai rapidement et me mis au lit, prenant avec moi, conformément à ma vieille habitude, un livre que je lisais généralement pour m'endormir. J'ouvris l'ouvrage dès que j'eus posé ma tête sur l'oreiller, et le jetai immédiatement de l'autre côté de la pièce. C'était *L'Histoire des monstres*, par Goudon, une étrange œuvre française, que j'avais récemment importée de Paris, mais qui, dans l'état d'esprit où je me trouvais ce soir là, était tout sauf un compagnon agréable. Je me résolus à dormir immédiatement, aussi, éteignant ma lampe à gaz jusqu'à ce que rien d'autre qu'un petit point bleu de lumière ne brillât au dessus du tuyau, je me préparai au repos une fois encore.

La chambre était plongée dans l'obscurité la plus totale. L'atome de gaz qui demeurait allumé n'éclairait pas plus de sept ou huit centimètres autour du brûleur. Dans un mouvement désespéré, je croisai les bras devant les yeux, comme pour les fermer à l'obscurité elle-même et essayai de ne penser à rien. Ce fut en vain. Les sujets déconcertants abordés par Hammond dans le jardin ne cessaient de s'imposer à mon cerveau. Je me battais contre eux. Je tentais d'ériger des remparts en mettant mon intelligence au repos pour les maintenir à distance. Mais ils persistaient à m'assaillir en nombre. Comme je gisais, pareil à un cadavre, espérant que, par une inaction physique parfaite, j'accélérerais le repos de l'esprit, un incident affreux se produisit. Une Chose tomba, sembla-t-il, du plafond, atterrit en plein sur ma poitrine et, l'instant d'après, je sentis deux mains osseuses serrer ma gorge, s'efforçant de m'étouffer.

Je ne manque pas de courage et suis doté d'une force physique considérable. La soudaineté de l'attaque, au lieu de m'abasourdir amena chacun de mes nerfs à son plus haut point de tension. Mon corps agit d'instinct, avant que mon cerveau n'eut le temps de réaliser les terreurs impliquées par ma situation. En un instant j'entourai la créature de deux bras musclés, et la pressai, avec toute la force du désespoir, contre ma poitrine. En quelques secondes, les mains osseuses qui s'étaient refermées sur ma gorge perdirent de leur emprise, et je fus libre de respirer à nouveau. Alors commença une lutte d'une affreuse intensité. Immergé dans l'obscurité la plus profonde, totalement ignorant de la nature de la Chose qui m'attaquait si soudainement, me rendant compte que je lâchais peu à peu prise, à cause, me semblait-il, de la nudité totale de mon assaillant, mordu par des dents pointues à l'épaule, au cou, et à la poitrine, devant à chaque instant protéger ma gorge d'une paire de mains vigoureuses et agiles que mes efforts les plus intenses n'arrivaient pas à contenir, je me trouvais face à un mélange de circonstances à combattre qui requéraient toute la force et toutes les capacités et tout le courage que je possédais.

Enfin, après une lutte silencieuse, implacable, épuisante, j'eus le dessus sur mon assaillant grâce à une série d'efforts incroyables. Une fois mon adversaire immobilisé avec mon genou sur ce qui me semblait être sa poitrine, je sus que j'étais le vainqueur. Je me reposai un instant pour reprendre ma respiration. J'entendis la créature haleter dans l'obscurité et ressentis le battement d'un cœur. Elle semblait plus épuisée que moi, cela me réconforta. À ce moment-là, je me souvins que j'avais pour habitude de placer sous mon oreiller, avant de me coucher, un grand mouchoir de poche en soie jaune, à utiliser pendant la nuit. Je le cherchai aussitôt du bout des doigts, il était bien là. Il me fallut quelques secondes de plus pour attacher, tant bien que mal, les bras de la créature.

Je me sentais désormais relativement en sécurité. Il n'y avait rien à faire de plus si ce n'était allumer la lumière, et, après avoir vu à quoi ressemblait mon assaillant de minuit, réveiller la maisonnée. J'admets bien volontiers que j'étais mû par une certaine fierté de n'avoir pas donné l'alerte plus tôt : je souhaitais faire la capture seul et sans l'aide de quiconque.

Ne relâchant à aucun moment mon emprise sur la créature, je me laissai glisser du lit au sol, entrainant le prisonnier dans ma chute. Je n'avais que quelques pas à faire pour atteindre la lampe à gaz. Ces pas, je les fis avec toute la prudence possible, tenant la créature de main ferme, comme serrée dans un étau. Je parvins enfin à portée de main de la minuscule tâche de lumière bleue qui m'indiquait la place du brûleur à gaz. Aussi rapide que l'éclair, je lâchai la créature d'une main et laissai toute la lumière s'échapper. Puis, je me tournai pour regarder mon prisonnier.

Il m'est impossible ne serait-ce que de tenter de définir mes sensations l'instant après avoir allumé la lampe. Je suppose que je dus pousser un hurlement de terreur, car, moins d'une minute après, ma chambre était envahie par les pensionnaires de la maison. Je tremble à présent en pensant à cet affreux moment. Je ne vis rien ! Oui, c'est bien cela, je tenais d'un bras ferme une forme qui respirait, qui haletait, qui avait tout d'un corps, mon autre main serrait de toutes ses forces une gorge aussi chaude, et visiblement aussi charnue que la mienne, et pourtant, avec cette substance vivante entre les mains, son corps pressé contre le mien, et tout cela dans l'éclat vif d'une grande lueur de gaz, je ne vis absolument rien ! Pas même une silhouette, une vapeur !

Je ne réalise point, aujourd'hui encore, la situation dans laquelle je me trouvai alors. Je ne peux me souvenir de cet étonnant incident de manière précise. Mon imagination essaie en vain de mesurer l'affreux paradoxe.

Cela respirait. Je sentais sa respiration chaude sur ma joue. Cela se battait avec rage. Cela avait des mains. Elles m'agrippaient. Sa peau était douce, exactement comme la mienne. Cela était couché là, serré tout contre moi, dur comme pierre, et pourtant totalement invisible !

Je me demande comment je ne m'évanouis ou ne perdis pas la raison sur le champ. Quelque instinct merveilleux dut me soutenir ; en effet, au lieu d'atténuer mon emprise sur la terrible Enigme, j'eus l'impression de gagner en force dans mon moment d'horreur et je serrai davantage et avec une force si extraordinaire, que je sentis la créature frissonner, à l'agonie.

Ce fut précisément à ce moment-là qu'Hammond entra dans ma chambre, suivi de tous les pensionnaires. Dès qu'il vit mon visage, qui je suppose, devait être un bien affreux spectacle, il s'avança précipitamment, en criant : « Mon Dieu, Harry, que s'est-il passé ?

—Hammond ! Hammond ! criai-je, venez ici. Oh, c'est affreux ! J'ai été attaqué dans mon lit par je ne sais quelle créature, que je tiens entre mes mains, mais je ne la vois pas, je ne la vois pas ! »

Hammond, sans aucun doute frappé par l'horreur sincère

que traduisait l'expression de mon visage, fit un ou deux pas en avant avec un air inquiet mais intrigué. Un petit rire sot très audible émana du reste de mes visiteurs. Cet éclat de rire retenu me mit hors de moi. Se moquer d'un être humain dans ma situation ! C'était de la cruauté de la pire espèce. Maintenant, je comprends en quoi l'apparence d'un homme luttant violemment contre ce qui apparaissait comme une créature faite d'air et appelant à l'aide contre une hallucination, pouvait paraitre ridicule. À ce moment-là, telle fut ma rage contre la foule moqueuse que, si j'en avais eu le pouvoir, je les aurais frappés à mort à l'endroit même où ils se tenaient.

« Hammond ! Hammond ! criai-je encore, désespéré, pour l'amour du ciel, venez donc! Je ne vais pas pouvoir tenir la... la Chose beaucoup plus longtemps. Elle est en train de me terrasser. Aidez-moi ! Aidez-moi !

—Harry, chuchota Hammond, en s'approchant de moi, vous avez fumé trop d'opium.

—Je vous jure Hammond que ce n'est pas une hallucination, répondis-je d'une même voix basse. Ne voyez-vous pas comme elle secoue tout mon corps en se débattant ? Si vous ne me croyez pas, vous n'avez qu'à vous en convaincre par vous-même : tâtez-la, touchez-la. »

Hammond s'avança et posa sa main à l'endroit que je lui indiquai. Un cri d'horreur, sauvage, s'échappa de lui. Il l'avait sentie !

En un instant, il avait trouvé quelque part dans ma chambre un long morceau de ficelle, et, la minute d'après, il l'enroulait et la nouait autour du corps de l'être invisible que je serrais dans mes bras.

« Harry, dit-il d'une voix rauque et agitée, car bien qu'il eût gardé tous ses esprits, il était profondément ému, Harry, il n'y a plus aucun danger à présent. Vous pouvez lâcher prise, mon vieux, si vous êtes fatigué. La Chose ne peut pas bouger. »

J'étais absolument épuisé et ce fut avec plaisir que je relâchai mon emprise.

Hammond resta debout à tenir les extrémités de la ficelle qui liait l'Invisible, enroulés autour de sa main, pendant que devant lui il regardait une corde lacée et entrelacée, tenant pour ainsi dire toute seule, bien serrée autour d'un espace vide. Je n'avais jamais vu un homme semblant à ce point saisi de stupeur. Néanmoins, son visage exprimait tout le courage et toute la détermination que je lui connaissais. Ses lèvres, bien que blanches, ne tremblaient pas et on pouvait percevoir d'un seul coup d'œil, que, quoique saisi d'effroi, il demeurait imperturbable.

La confusion qui s'ensuivit parmi les pensionnaires de la maison, qui furent les témoins de cette scène extraordinaire entre Hammond et moi-même, qui virent le pantomime qui consistait à lier cette Chose qui se débattait, qui me virent près de m'écrouler d'épuisement physique lorsque ma tâche de geôlier prit fin ; la confusion et la terreur qui s'emparèrent des spectateurs, lorsqu'ils virent tout cela, allaient au delà de toute description. Plusieurs, parmi les plus faibles, s'enfuirent de l'appartement. Les rares qu'ils laissèrent derrière eux se regroupèrent près de la porte, et il fut impossible de les convaincre d'approcher Hammond et sa Charge. Néanmoins, l'incrédulité transparaissait dans leur terreur. Ils n'avaient point le courage de s'assurer de ce qu'ils voyaient et cependant ils doutaient. Ce fut en vain que je suppliai certains des hommes présents de s'approcher et de constater de leurs propres mains l'existence d'un être vivant invisible dans cette chambre. Ils étaient incrédules mais n'osaient point se détromper. Comment un corps solide, vivant et qui respirait pouvait-il être invisible? demandèrent-ils. Ma réponse fut la suivante. Je fis signe à Hammond, et, ensemble, chacun de nous vainquant son effrayante répugnance à toucher la créature invisible, nous la levâmes du sol, menottée comme elle l'était, et la portâmes sur mon lit. Son poids était approximativement celui d'un garçon de quatorze ans. « À présent, mes amis, dis-je, comme Hammond et moi-même tenions la créature suspendue au-dessus du lit, je peux vous donner une preuve évidente que voici un corps plein, pondérable, que vous ne voyez néanmoins pas. Veuillez avoir l'obligeance de regarder attentivement la surface du lit. »

Je fus étonné de mon propre courage, celui qui consistait à faire face à cet étrange événement avec autant de calme ; mais je m'étais remis de ma terreur initiale et l'affaire me faisait éprouver une sorte de fierté scientifique qui dominait tout autre sentiment.

Les yeux des spectateurs fixèrent immédiatement mon lit. À un signal donné, Hammond et moi laissâmes la créature tomber. On entendit le bruit sourd d'un corps lourd atterrissant sur une masse moelleuse. Le bois du lit crissa. Une empreinte profonde se dessina distinctement sur l'oreiller et sur le lit lui-même. La foule qui fut le témoin de cela poussa une sorte de cri étouffé et général et se précipita hors de la chambre. Hammond et moi nous retrouvâmes seuls avec notre Mystère.

Nous restâmes silencieux pendant un certain temps, à écouter la respiration basse et irrégulière de la créature sur le lit, et à regarder le mouvement des draps alors qu'elle luttait, impuissante, pour se libérer de ses liens. Puis Hammond parla : « Harry, c'est affreux.

—Oui, affreux.

—Mais pas inexplicable.

—Comment cela, pas inexplicable ! Que voulez-vous dire ? Une telle chose ne s'est jamais produite depuis la naissance du monde. Je ne sais que penser, Hammond. Puisse Dieu m'assurer que je ne suis pas fou et que ceci n'est point un fantasme délirant.

—Réfléchissons un peu, Harry. Voici un corps plein que nous touchons, mais que nous ne voyons pas. Le fait est si inhabituel qu'il nous frappe de terreur. N'y a-t-il pas de parallèle, cependant, à ce phénomène ? Prenez un morceau de verre pur. C'est quelque chose de tangible et transparent. Une certaine grossièreté chimique est tout ce qui l'empêche d'être entièrement transparent au point d'en être totalement invisible. Il n'est pas théoriquement impossible, remarquez, de fabriquer un verre qui ne reflétera pas un seul rayon de lumière, un verre si pur et homogène dans ses atomes que les rayons du soleil passeront à travers comme ils le font à travers l'air, réfracté mais pas reflété. Nous ne voyons pas l'air, et pourtant nous le sentons.

—Tout ceci est bien joli, Hammond, mais il s'agit de substances inanimées. Le verre ne respire pas, l'air ne respire pas. Cette chose a un cœur qui palpite. Une volonté qui la fait se mouvoir. Des poumons qui jouent et inspirent et respirent.

—Vous oubliez les étranges phénomènes dont nous avons si souvent entendu parler ces derniers temps, répondit le docteur avec gravité. Aux réunions appelées « tables tournantes », des mains invisibles ont été glissées dans celles de ces personnes réunies autour de la table—des mains chaudes, de chair, qui semblaient vibrer de vie mortelle.

—Quoi ? Pensez-vous, alors, que cette chose est ...

—J'ignore ce que c'est, fut sa réponse solennelle ; mais plaise aux dieux qu'avec votre aide, je cherche à le savoir de manière approfondie. »

Nous passâmes toute la nuit au chevet de la créature venue d'une autre planète, à l'observer ensemble, tout en fumant de nombreuses pipes. Elle s'agita et haleta jusqu'à paraître à bout de forces. Puis, nous apprîmes par sa respiration faible, régulière qu'elle dormait. Le lendemain matin, la maison était en émoi. Les pensionnaires s'étaient rassemblés sur le palier de ma chambre, et Hammond et moi-même étions des lions. Nous eûmes à répondre à mille questions concernant l'état de notre extraordinaire prisonnier, car, à ce moment-là, à part nous, nul dans la maison ne se laissa convaincre de mettre les pieds dans l'appartement.

La créature était éveillée. La manière convulsive avec laquelle elle faisait remuer les draps dans ses efforts pour échapper en attestait. Il y avait quelque-chose de vraiment terrible dans le fait de regarder, en quelque sorte, ces indications de seconde main de ses terribles torsions et de ses mouvements de lutte désespérés pour la liberté, qui eux-mêmes étaient invisibles.

Durant la longue nuit, Hammond et moi-même nous étions creusé la tête pour découvrir quelque moyen par lequel il nous serait peut-être possible de prendre conscience de la forme et de l'apparence d'ensemble de l'Enigme. Pour autant que nous pouvions le distinguer en passant nos mains sur la silhouette de la créature, ses contours et ses caractéristiques étaient humains. Il y avait une bouche ; une tête, ronde, lisse et chauve, un nez, qui cependant se trouvait à peine au-dessus des joues ; et ses mains et ses pieds rappelaient ceux d'un garçon. Dans un premier temps, nous envisageâmes de placer l'être sur une surface lisse et d'en tracer le contour avec de la craie, comme les cordonniers le font avec le contour du pied. Ce plan fut abandonné car jugé inutile. Un tel tracé n'eut pas donné la moindre idée de la structure de la créature.

Je fus saisi d'une pensée heureuse. Nous en ferions un moulage avec du plâtre à mouler. Ceci nous révélerait la silhouette dans sa texture et satisferait tous nous souhaits. Mais comment le faire ? Les mouvements de la créature perturberaient le durcissement de l'enveloppe malléable et déformeraient le moule. Une autre pensée. Pourquoi ne pas la soumettre au chloroforme ? Elle avait des organes respiratoires—sa respiration en était la preuve. Une fois réduite à un état d'insensibilité, nous pourrions faire d'elle ce que nous voudrions. On fit venir le docteur X ; et après que le vénérable médecin se fût remis de sa stupéfaction initiale, il entreprit de lui administrer le chloroforme. Trois minutes après nous fumes en mesure de retirer les entraves du corps de la créature, et un modeleur célèbre de la ville fut très occupé à enduire la forme invisible d'argile humide. Il nous fallut cinq minutes de plus pour avoir un moule et, avant le soir, un facsimile approximatif du Mystère. Il avait la forme d'un homme.

Difforme, grossier, et horrible, mais un homme bel et bien. Il était petit, pas plus d'un mètre quarante environ de hauteur, et ses membres traduisaient un développement musculaire sans égal. Son visage dépassait en laideur tout ce que j'avais pu voir jusqu'alors. Gustave Doré, ou Jacques Callot ou encore Tony Johannot ne conçurent jamais rien d'aussi horrible. Il y a un visage, dans une illustration réalisée par ce dernier pour *Un Voyage où il vous plaira* qui se rapproche quelque peu de l'expression de cette créature, mais ne l'égale pas. C'était ainsi que j'imaginais la physionomie d'un vampire. Il semblait capable de se nourrir de chair humaine.

Une fois notre curiosité satisfaite, et toute la maisonnée liée au secret, la question se posa de savoir que faire de l'Enigme. Il n'était pas possible de garder une telle horreur dans notre maison ; il était tout aussi impossible de laisser en liberté un être aussi affreux. Je confesse que j'aurais volontiers voté pour la destruction de la créature. Mais qui devrait endosser la responsabilité ? Qui se chargerait d'exécuter cet horrible semblant d'être humain ? Jour après jour, cette question fut l'objet de débats menés avec gravité. Tous les pensionnaires quittèrent la maison. Mrs Moffat était au désespoir, et nous menaça, Hammond et moi-même, de toutes sortes de pénalités légales si nous ne nous débarrassions pas de l'Horreur. Notre réponse fut la suivante : « Nous partirons si tel est votre souhait, mais nous refusons d'emporter cette créature avec nous. Enlevez-la vous même si cela vous chante. Elle est apparue dans votre maison. La responsabilité repose donc sur vous-même » À ceci, bien sûr, il n'y eut point de réponse. Mrs Moffat ne put obtenir pour rien au monde que quelqu'un ne fît ne serait-ce qu'approcher le Mystère.

La partie la plus singulière de la transaction fut que nous

ignorions totalement de quoi la créature avait coutume de se nourrir. Nous plaçâmes devant elle tout ce qu'il nous fut possible d'imaginer en termes de nourriture, mais rien ne fut jamais touché. C'était affreux de rester là, jour après jour, et de voir les tissus s'agiter et d'entendre la respiration haletante, et de savoir qu'elle mourait de faim.

Dix jours, douze jours, quinze jours passèrent, et elle vivait toujours. Les battements du cœur, néanmoins, faiblissaient de jour en jour et avaient à ce stade presque complètement cessé. Il ne faisait aucun doute que la créature était en train de mourir de faim. Tout le temps que dura cette terrible lutte pour la vie, j'étais au plus mal. Je n'arrivais plus à trouver le sommeil. Aussi horrible que fût la créature, penser aux souffrances qu'elle endurait faisait pitié.

Enfin, elle mourut. Hammond et moi la trouvâmes froide et raide dans le lit, un matin. Le cœur avait cessé de battre, les poumons de fonctionner. Nous nous empressâmes de l'enterrer dans le jardin. Ce fut un étrange enterrement, de laisser tomber ce cadavre invisible dans le trou humide. Le moulage de sa forme, je le donnai au docteur X, qui le conserve dans son musée sur Tenth Street.

Alors que je suis sur le point d'entamer un long voyage dont je pourrais ne jamais revenir, j'ai élaboré ce récit de l'événement le plus singulier qu'il me fut donné à connaître.

Note : La rumeur veut que les propriétaires d'un musée célèbre de la ville aient convenu avec docteur X de présenter au public le moulage singulier que Mr Escott lui confia. Une histoire aussi extraordinaire ne peut qu'attirer l'attention de tous.

How Much of a Man is Three Fifths of a Man?

Fitz-James O'Brien & the Dred Scott Decision[1]

Dr Kristine Hoyt Jouanne

February 16, 1862, in the state of West Virginia, a brilliant young Irish poet leads his cavalry on a daring charge against Confederate soldiers. He takes a bullet through the upper chest, but even with blood pouring from his wound, he continues his charge, encouraging his men forward until he is finally taken to the rear by a subordinate who realizes that he is about to fall off his horse from loss of blood.[2] Less than two months later, ten years after immigrating to New York, Lieutenant Fitz-James O'Brien, Company 7 of the United States Volunteers, succumbs to his wounds, dead at the age of 33. Small comfort were the words of commendation he received for his "gallantry in service" from none other than Union General George B. McClellan.[3]

In this essay I will share some thoughts about this Irishman from County Cork who not only fought and died so valiantly in the American Civil War but who was also instrumental in the development of American literature, particularly the short story, science fiction, and tales of the supernatural. I will focus on how his 1859 short story 'What Was It? A Mystery' about an invisible, not quite human creature intertwines with the 1857 *Dred Scott vs Sandford* Supreme Court decision, and conclude by exploring how this is connected with science fiction and the supernatural.

First of all, who was Dred Scott? Dred Scott was a slave who had been suing his owners for his freedom since 1846 based on the fact that he had been living in free territory. His case made its way to the United States Supreme Court whose 1857 decision was highly controversial, outraging Northerners and abolitionists: not only did it refuse Scott's case for emancipation from slavery but it made slavery a national institution instead of a local one, meaning it was an all but constitutional right to own other "human" beings. This firmly established that those not quite human creatures of African descent were to be considered first and foremost as property.[4] I believe that O'Brien's short story about an invisible not quite human creature, of about three-fifths the size of an average-sized man, can be read as an allegory to the Dred Scott decision and the Three-Fifths Compromise of Article One Section Two Paragraph Three of the Constitution used to count blacks for representation purposes.

I will begin with some context about what was happening in America in the 1850s and about the road to Civil War. The Great Potato Famine had caused a massive influx of Irish immigrants into the Northern cities. These poor immigrants were often ill-treated, called white negroes by some, the "missing link" by others, and generally discriminated against: "Irish need not apply."[5] By certain accounts, even if O'Brien played on positive Irish stereotypes in his favour, he was "profoundly ashamed to be Irish" and avoided all contact with his lower-class countrymen. Because of the airs he took, his associates nicknamed him "the Baron," but he was still Irish underneath.

It was 19th century America and the East was filling up, but Americans were on the move and they were heading west. What for 200 years had been a trickle barely making it beyond the Mississippi River was turning into a flood of pioneers eager to brave the arduous trip west across lands that no whites had ever even set eyes on before Lewis and Clark began their great exploration of the Louisiana Territory in 1804. The December 2, 1823 Monroe Doctrine stated that further efforts by European countries to colonize land or interfere with states in the Americas would be viewed as acts of aggression requiring U.S. intervention. The Monroe Doctrine also asserted that although the Americas were not to be further colonized by European countries, the United States would not interfere with existing European colonies either. Shortly thereafter, Americans started interfering in Texas which had been first Spanish, then Mexican. Remember the Alamo? That was in 1836 and was wholly illegal. Nonetheless, within a decade, Texas had been annexed. In 1845, New York journalist John O'Sullivan wrote, "Nothing must interfere with the fulfilment of our manifest destiny to overspread the continent allotted by Providence for the free development of our yearly multiplying millions."[6] In 1848 gold was discovered in California and the Rush was on. By 1850 California and Texas were states; Oregon, New Mexico, and Utah were territories; and the Great Plains were open to settlement.

So what has westward expansion to do with Fitz-James O'Brien, Dred Scott, and the Civil War? To put it simply, this Westward expansion called into question the expansion of slavery as well. Were these new territories to be slave states or free states? If they were free, would slave owners be able to travel there with their slaves? If they were free, and outnumbered the slave states in Congress, would the South be outnumbered? Was total emancipation peeping over the horizon? For most politicians it was a moot point because these territories were unlike the deep South and were considered ill-suited to slavery. Politics and morals and very high emotions were involved, however, and so in 1850 a compromise was reached which: 1) reinforced the Fugitive Slave Act meaning that with the slightest proof, a Southerner could travel to the North and recuperate his property, no questions asked; 2) California would be a Free State and Texas a Slave State; 3) The Slave Trade would be abolished in the District of Columbia; and 4) the new Territories would have sovereignty to decide amongst themselves what they would do, once again avoiding the moral question. This turned into a mess, of course. In the North, when Southerners came to claim runaway slaves there were riots. The territory of Kansas became known as "Bleeding Kansas" for the fighting and killing between pro- and anti-slavery forces "choosing amongst themselves."

The South felt it needed slavery and that it was justified in its "peculiar institution,"[7] some even arguing that it was better to be a slave than a poor, white immigrant worker (read, Irish). Those against slavery in the North had thought that although they were on the moral high ground, against slavery, slavery in the south was not *their* responsibility—IT WAS SOMEBODY ELSE'S PROBLEM. Morally, they considered themselves to be blameless, because they themselves did not own slaves. This position was getting increasingly difficult to maintain, however, and the abolitionist movement was growing. In 1852, the year of Fitz-James O'Brien's arrival in America, *Uncle Tom's Cabin* came out and sold 300,000 copies in just one year. America's northern literati of Emerson, Thoreau, Melville, the Alcotts, Walt Whitman, Whittier, Oliver Wendell Holmes, and many others were anti-slavery. The movement was growing. Frederick Douglass, the charismatic and eloquent former slave, stood before white audiences in the North and told them: "slavery brands your republicanism as a sham, your humanity as a base pretence, and your Christianity as a lie."[8] Things were coming to a head—the problem was not going to sort itself out. Abraham Lincoln who had been "realistic" about slavery and the difficulties involved in full emancipation had his own moral epiphany in 1854, which was to become his guiding light: "If slavery is not wrong, then nothing is wrong." Working in the world of journalism and thanks to the people he was frequenting, Fitz-James O'Brien was fully aware of what was going on around him.

During this time, Dred Scott had been trying to sue for his freedom, arguing that he had been living in free states with his master, and, because they were free states, he should be free. The case reached the Supreme Court and the decision they handed down was a slap in the face to the Abolitionists and Northerners in general. The decision was based on the fifth amendment of the Bill of Rights:

> (...) an act of Congress which deprives a person of his freedom or his property merely because he travels or takes his property into a particular Territory can hardly be dignified with the name of due process by law.

The Justices were not talking about Dred Scott's freedom, but of his owners' right to move their chattel freely wherever they wished. They also decided that Dred Scott did not even have the right to come before the court because even though he was born in the USA he was not, nor ever would he be, a citizen of the United States due to his African ancestry. The Court also presented a parade of horrible arguments as to the feared results of granting Mr Scott's petition:

> It would give to persons of the negro race, (...) the right to enter every other State whenever they pleased, (...) the full liberty of speech in public and in private upon all subjects upon which its own citizens might speak; to hold public meetings upon political affairs, and to keep and carry arms wherever they went.

Their interpretation was based on what they imagined the Founding Fathers would have thought, this based on Article One Section Two Paragraph Three of the American Constitution stating:

> Representatives and direct Taxes shall be apportioned among the several States which may be included within this Union, according to their respective Numbers, which shall be determined by adding to the whole Number of free Persons, including those bound to Service for a Term of Years, and excluding Indians not taxed, three fifths of all other Persons.

This meant that men of African descent counted as "almost" men. They were used for white representation but had no voice nor vote of their own.

Now back to our Civil War hero Fitz-James O'Brien. Our young man was born in County Cork to a wealthy land-owning family in 1828. He inherited his paternal grandfather's estate when he was still a baby and his father's when he was fourteen years old. His mother remarried and he moved with her and his step-father to an estate overlooking the Shannon river in Limerick. He was raised a gentleman, and partook of the activities of his class: he hunted, fished, watched birds, wrote lyrical poetry, but was not indifferent to the calamity that had hit those around him. He was sensitive to the plight of the poor Irish during the early stages of the Famine and wrote two poems that were published in the *Nation*: 'Oh give a desert life to me' where he speaks of fleeing to America where he would be free of the tyrant's rule and returning when "Old Erin's chain is cleft by freemen's swords in two." The following year he published 'The Famine' warning of impending riots if the suffering of the poor was not alleviated. His concern for his fellow Irish did not prevent him from picking up and moving to London—land of the vile Oppressor—when he came of age and inherited his money. This would not be the last of the contradictions in his behaviour. After squandering his money and possibly getting into trouble with the wrong woman (reports on this phase of his life are vague), he left for America.

In early 1852 he arrived in New York City with letters of introduction to New York social circles in one pocket and only $60 in the other. Through his connections he found magazine and journal work, and established himself as the popular columnist "The Man about Town." He and his new friends held forth at a place called Pfaff's Beer Cellar, and called themselves Bohemians after French writer Henri Murger's *Scènes de la Vie de Bohème* (1841-42). He mixed and mingled with other writers, actors, and the intelligentsia of the time, who were also more or less vocal about their anti-slavery sentiments. From the beginning of his time in America until his death, he wrote poems, essays, plays, and columns that were lyrical, gossipy, witty, and/or literary, but also concerned with societal ills. A reason for this could be that in America he discovered what it was like to be a starving artist living like a starving labourer in a nasty tenement not knowing where the next meal would be coming from. At any rate, he wrote extensively about the slums, the tenement buildings, the women who slaved to make cheap clothing for low pay. This was one of his pet subjects: he wrote frequently about seamstresses and the low pay they received for their work, for example: 'The Shirt Fiend, A Christmas Carol'[9] or 'The Spectral Shirt.'[10] Feeling sorry for these women did not stop him from buying their dollar shirts, however. The poem 'An Old Story'[11] tells the tale of an old prostitute who wanders through the snow, alone and miserable, until she reaches the home of the man who had abandoned her to the streets:

> And lifeless she falls at the outer gate
> Of him who has left her desolate

The snow gently covers her "as though God in His mercy had willed that she should die in a garment of purity." And, thus, beneath the snow, she becomes *invisible*. In 'The Beggar Child'[12] from his series *Street Lyrics* he tells of a rich man who absolutely does not believe the stories of abject poverty in New York until he meets an emaciated, bare-footed beggar child who takes him to the squalid tenement where his widowed mother is sewing shirts for money to feed her five children. This is a revelation to the man for whom these people had been *invisible*. He decides to use his money to help relieve the suffering of the poor and hungry whom he had never seen before.

This leads us to the subject of social invisibility. This is Ralph Ellison's *Invisible Man* (1952) as opposed to H .G. Wells' *Invisible Man* (1897): the former is a commentary on what it is like to be a black man in 1950s America, whereas the latter is science fiction. In the 1970s Douglas Adams coined the term "SEP" which combines both notions of social invisibility and science fiction. An SEP is Someone Else's Problem (like Southern slavery to Northerners), and in his *Hitch Hiker's Guide to the Galaxy* series he explains it like this:

> An SEP (...) is something we can't see, or don't see, or our brain doesn't let us see, because we think that it's somebody else's problem (...) The brain just edits it out, it's like a blind spot. If you look at it directly you won't see it unless you know precisely what it is. Your only hope is to catch it by surprise out of the corner of your eye.[13]

The technology used to make people and things invisible is so complex and unreliable that it is not worth the bother. On the other hand,

> the Somebody Else's Problem field is much simpler and more effective, and can be run for over a hundred years on a single torch battery. This is because it relies on people's natural predisposition not to see anything they don't want to, weren't expecting, or can't explain.[14]

This is the phenomenon at work in Poe's 'Purloined Letter' (1844): the stolen letter is impossible to find because it is OUT IN PLAIN VIEW! In other words, instead of the object of affliction disappearing, it remains, but cannot be perceived because it has become somebody else's problem, somebody else's job to take care of it. Your only hope to see it is to catch it by surprise out of the corner of your eye, or have it catch you by surprise, as it does when it drops on Harry Escott in the middle of the night and tries to strangle him.

'What Was It?' is O'Brien's second Harry Escott tale which gives Harry credibility within the tale itself because of his prior experience with the supernatural:

> I found myself a person of immense importance, it having leaked out that I was tolerably well-versed in the history of supernaturalism, and had once written a story the foundation of which was a ghost.[15]

As the story was written in the first person and was so credible, *Harper's Magazine* received multiple letters addressed to "Harry Escott." The first ghost story was the 'Pot of Tulips'[16] and was about injustice on a personal level. Ghosts appear to Harry in the night to help him right a wrong.

In 'What Was It?' no wrong will be righted. On the contrary, a creature is left to starve to death, frightened and alone. In this story, Harry Escott is in bed trying to sleep after having smoked a good deal of opium, when an invisible creature drops from the ceiling and lands on him. It tries to choke Harry but he overpowers and captures it, then has to convince the others in his boarding house that he's holding a real creature. To prove to the other boarders that this creature exists he and his friend decide to drop it on the bed: "I can give you *self-evident* proof that here is a solid ponderable body, which, nevertheless, you cannot see."[17] Do you hear an echo of the second sentence of the Declaration of Independence?

> We hold these truths to be *self-evident*, that all men are created equal, that they are endowed by their Creator with certain unalienable rights, that among these are Life, Liberty and the Pursuit of Happiness.[18]

This self-evident truth was much discussed at the time: in 1855 Abraham Lincoln expressed his alarm that the pro-slavery, anti-immigrant Know-Nothing party might come into power: "If they were in power the Declaration of Independence would read "all men are created equal, except negroes, and foreigners, and Catholics." Female abolitionist Abby Kelley wrote "We have good reason to be grateful to the slave. In striving to strike his irons off, we found most surely, that we were manacled ourselves." In 1848 at the Seneca Falls Women's Convention, a "Declaration of Sentiments" was drafted stating: "We hold these truths to be self-evident: that all men and women are created equal."[19]

Now, returning to our story, Harry and his doctor friend are at a loss as to what to do with their captive:

> There was something truly terrible in beholding, as it were, those second-hand indications of the terrible writhings and agonized struggles for *liberty* which themselves were invisible.[20]

Let's look for a moment at how this creature is described. In the text, capital letters are used to name it, since they don't know what it is: a Something, the Thing, the terrible Enigma, the Invisible, the Charge, the Horror, the Mystery. It's an IT, a what, not a human, not a who. Yet, from the first encounter Harry feels that it has skin like him, that it has the weight and size of a 14-year old boy, and that it "has a heart that palpitates—a will that moves it—lungs that play, and inspire and respire."[21]

When they make a cast of it they see that it has the physiognomy of a flat-nosed "ghoul" and conjecture out of fear that it might just eat human flesh. They also see to what extent it has the semblance of a human being. If you consider the caricatures of blacks and Irish produced at that time, you will get an idea of how monstrous such a creature could look.[22] Harry and the doctor contemplate what should be done with their captive. Harry admits that he would have gladly voted for its "destruction," but no one—out of squeamishness rather than conviction—will agree to execute this "fac-simile" of a human being. And even though the creature is more hideous than anything he has ever seen, Harry starts to feel sorry for it—he and the doctor give it everything they can think of to try and feed it, but it eats nothing. They try everything, except of course, removing its fetters and liberating it.

> It was awful to stand by day after day and see the clothes toss and hear the hard breathing and know that it was starving [...]. While this terrible life-struggle was going on I felt miserable. I could not sleep. Horrible as the creature was, it was pitiful to think of the pangs it was suffering. At last it died. We hastened to bury it in the garden.[23]

This haste makes us feel—and share—their guilt and shame. They had preferred to let it die, rather than let it go.

Civil War was coming and questions were being asked about the nature of these people from Africa and what was to be done with them. The Northern States had been content as long as slavery was contained in the South, but new states were going to join the union, would they be free or slave? It had been that if a slave arrived in the north he was granted freedom, and what's more, at the time of the drafting of the Constitution black men could vote in ten out of thirteen states. What had happened? By looking the other way, were the Northerners tacitly complicit, aiding and abetting? Then came Dred Scott in 1857 and the Supreme Court's decision that the United States Congress had no authority to prohibit slavery in federal territories. The Court also ruled that because slaves were not and could never be citizens, they could never sue in court—they would never be heard. Lastly, the Court ruled that slaves were chattel— their owners could shackle them, do what they would. They were

> beings of an inferior order, and altogether unfit to associate with the white race, either in social or political relations, and so far inferior that they had no rights which the white man was bound to respect.[24]

As we have seen, for all intents and purposes, one black man counted as three fifths of a white man, which gave his owners more representative clout in government but himself no voice. He was psychologically and metaphorically stunted, invisible to the Law, and to Society. Instead of settling once and for all the slavery question, this decision served to galvanize the North and the Abolitionists. 'What Was It?'was published in March of 1859. In October of that year came John Brown and the Harpers Ferry slave uprising. In 1860 Lincoln was elected and in February of '61, the South voted unanimously to secede. On April 12, 1861 shots were fired at Fort Sumter, the War was on, and Fitz-James O'Brien was a volunteer in the 7th Regiment.

To make one last connection between social commentary and the supernatural element of Fitz-James O'Brien's tale, I will discuss another movement that was at large at the time. It had crystallized in 1848 when Kate and Margaret Fox of upstate New York reported that they had made contact with the dead—the spirit communicated through rapping noises that onlookers could hear, like those in the boarding house where Harry and the doctor were living before the apparition of the creature. "The evidence of the senses appealed to practically-minded Americans." Harry says to his neighbours that he can give them "self-evident proof" that his invisible creature exists by dropping it on the bed. This movement was called Spiritualism and Harry's doctor friend makes a direct allusion to it in the text:

> You forget the phenomena of which we have so often heard of late," answered the doctor gravely. "At the meetings called 'spirit circles,' invisible hands have been thrust into the hands of those persons round the table–warm fleshly hands that seemed to pulsate with mortal life.[25]

Spiritualism was linked with Transcendentalism, whose followers were abolitionists. As we know, O'Brien travelled in these same literary and social circles. Spiritualism was a movement whose greatest followers came from the middle- and upper-classes, with women playing a prominent role. They believed that after death we progressed through various spheres and that the afterlife could not be reduced to the Heaven/Hell dichotomy. They believed that it was possible to communicate with the spirits of discarnate humans and that spirit mediums possessed the gift to do this. They believed that spirits were capable of growth and perfection. The afterlife was not a static place, but one in which spirits evolved.

The two beliefs—that contact with spirits was possible, and that spirits existed on a higher plane—led to a third belief: that spirits could provide knowledge about moral and ethical issues, as well as about God and the afterlife. Thus, many members spoke of spirit guides—specific spirits, often contacted, and relied upon for worldly and spiritual guidance. This was a movement based in Christianity. Members had become disillusioned with the organized churches that were not based enough on the New Testament, and were not concerned enough with social problems, in other words with Abolition, Women's Rights, Suffrage, drinking, cruelty to animals, workers' rights and so on. Interestingly, this is one of the many religious movements to come out of upstate New York's "burned-over" district during the Second Great Awakening. This district was also known for social radicalism, utopianism, vegetarianism, animal rights campaigns, and temperance, as well as abolition. Fitz-James O'Brien had visited this area and knew a great deal about the movement. Spiritualism is, then, the link between the social and the supernatural. We forget today how powerful it was at the time—even Mary Todd Lincoln was an adherent—and O'Brien was riding its wave and knew that his female readers would be there with him.

In symbolic form, as a caricature of a black man with three-fifths legal stature, the Creature could be from another plane—not another planet—there to give help to Harry with the moral and ethical issues facing him and those of his time. What does Harry do? Shackle the creature and let it die. If he did not learn the lesson, maybe his readers would? Maybe they will be struck by the dispassionate way in which rational men discuss what will happen to their "almost human" captive as they keep him in fetters and withhold his liberty. They stand by and watch the"invisible" suffering until "it" dies. Let's remember the poem young Fitz-James O'Brien had written as a teenager against English oppression of the Irish, dreaming of a life "amongst Columbia's free born race":

My soul is longing to be free,
Without the weight of chains it bore—
But when again Old Erin's chain,
is cleft by freemen's swords in two,
The sea I'll brave, and o'er the wave,
I'll come again dear land to you[26].

But he never did. He died in America, fighting to cleave in two the chains of another.

Notes

1 This essay deals with symbolism, metaphor, and artistic licence—it does not delve into the ideological debate involved in the interpretation of how racist (or not) the Three-Fifths compromise was and still is.

2 Francis Wolle, *Fitz-James O'Brien: A Literary Bohemian of the Eighteen-Fifties.* Boulder: University of Colorado Press, 1944, p.238. I am extremely indebted to Francis Wolle for his excellent biography of Fitz-James O'Brien.

3 *Ibid.*, p.239.

4 For further information on and reaction to the Dred Scott Decision, see Paul Finkleman, *Scott vs. Sandford: A Brief History with Documents* (1997); Earl M. Maltz, *Dred Scott and the Politics of Slavery* (2007); Ethan Greenberg, *Dred Scott and the Dangers of a Political Court* (2010).

5 For an excellent discussion of anti-Irish racism before, during, and after the Famine, please refer to the Ireland First website (eirefirst.com) under the headings "Irish Famine," then "Racism." The Anglo-Saxon comparisons between Africans and Celts are acute and damning. See also W.E.B. Dubois' *Black Folk Then and Now* discussing how the Irish were sold by the English as slaves in Barbados, with Irish women being "bred" to African-descent slaves to increase their numbers.

6 From 'Annexation' , *United States Magazine and Democratic Review*, 1845

7 James C. Calhoun, who served the United States as Vice President, Secretary of State, Senator and Representative during the first half of the19th century, referred to slavery as "a positive good" as opposed to "a necessary evil."

8 Frederick Douglass, *Select Addresses of Frederick Douglass*. New York: Wilder Publications, 2008, p.20.

9 *The Lantern*, April 24, 1852.

10 *Ibid.*, June 5, 1852.

11 *Ibid.*, April 17, 1852.

12 *Ibid.*, May 1, 1852..

13 Douglas Adams, *Life, the Universe and Everything.* London: Serious Productions Ltd, 1982, pp.26-27.

14 *Ibid.*, 33.

15 'What Was It?', p.6.

16 *Harper's Magazine*, XI, November 1855.

17 'What Was It?', p.15-16. All Italics now and hereafter are mine.

Notes

18 Here is a reminder of the first sentence of the Declaration of Independence: "When in the Course of human events, it becomes necessary for one people to dissolve the political bonds which have connected them with another, and to assume among the powers of the earth, the separate and equal station to which the Laws of Nature and of Nature's God entitle them, a decent respect to the opinions of mankind requires that they should declare the causes which impel them to the separation."

19 See the website *The Antislavery Literature Project* under the heading "legacies," then, "Frederick Douglass (Elizabeth Cady Stanton)" for further information and resources concerning Abolitionists and Suffragists working together.

20 'What Was It?'. p.18.

21 *Ibid.*, p.17.

22 See also the African and Irishman below. This illustration orginally appeared in H. Stricland Constable's *Ireland from One or Two Neglected Points of View* in 1899 and was reproduced in *Harper's Weekly* the same year.

IRISH IBERIAN ANGLO-TEUTONIC NEGRO

23 'What Was It?'. p.20.

24 In his remarks on the Dred Scott case, Chief Justice Taney is justifying the Court's ruling by using his interpretation of the prevailing attitude toward "that unfortunate race" at the time the Constitution was written.

25 'What Was It?'. p.17.

26 Printed in the Dublin weekly, the *Nation*, March 15, 1845. It was published to make the point that a good Irishman should stay and fight, not run away.

Seeing the Unseen:
Creating a Biology and Biome for Fitz-James O'Brien's Invisible Ghoul

Feargus Gwynplaine MacIntyre

I was about sixteen years old when I first encountered Fitz-James O'Brien's story 'What Was It? A Mystery'. The story had its intended effect of horrifying me, yet the story also left me unnerved for quite another reason. Here we have the account of a man living in the urban certainty of nineteenth-century Manhattan, safe in his bedroom with the door closed, when he is suddenly attacked by an invisible ghoul. When I first read this story, I had never yet visited the United States, yet I was reasonably certain that residents of Manhattan —in the nineteenth century, or any other—are not normally prey to attacks by invisible ghouls. If I were to suspend disbelief and accept this story as an actual event, then it would create a widening ripple of other questions. If one such attack can occur, then why are there not other reports of humans attacked by invisible ghouls? And how was this ghoul able to enter the narrator's bedroom without being heard? Some monsters—such as ghosts and vampires—are intangible, and can come and go as they please. O'Brien's ghoul is clearly all too tangible: when its hands are securely bound by the narrator, it is unable to free itself.

Clearly, O'Brien's ghoul represented some sort of an anomaly; a violation of our planet's usual rules. If the Abominable Snowman and the Loch Ness Monster are real, we can be certain that they are part of our planet Earth's biome; that they evolved as natural denizens of our own planet, and that they fulfil their roles as part of our planet's ecological order. O'Brien's invisible ghoul, on the other hand, is not part of our planet's business as usual. To quote the narrator of O'Brien's tale:

> Such a thing has never occurred since the birth of the world.

Clearly, O'Brien's mysterious ghoul is an alien in the true sense of that term: it is not a missing link from our own world, but rather a link from some alien food chain.

And yet there are different sorts of anomalies. We know that Frankenstein's monster is the only one of his kind, because we know how he came to be created, and we know that his creator never fully repeated the procedure. Was O'Brien's ghoul deliberately created as the homunculus of some mad alchemist? We have no evidence for this. More likely, the ghoul evolved as a typical member of its species. But if such a species exists, then where are this ghoul's cousins and siblings? Why are there no other reports of similar attacks upon unsuspecting humans?

Shortly after I first read O'Brien's story, I also encountered Guy de Maupassant's story 'The Horla'. Here too is an account of a commonplace man of our own world, strangely attacked by an invisible alien being. Could this be another account of the same phenomenon that occurred in O'Brien's tale? Ultimately, I think not. Apart from being invisible and predatory, the Horla in de Maupassant's story has almost nothing in common with O'Brien's ghoul, and I believe that they are two entirely different phenomena, from two different places.

When I was about nineteen years old, I discovered the writings of the American author Ambrose Bierce. One of his most famous works is his short story 'The Damned Thing', in which a nineteenth-century backwoodsman is attacked, mutilated and killed by an invisible creature. Here, at last, is a report of a creature on our own Earth that might be biologically related to O'Brien's ghoul. And yet there is a crucial difference: in Bierce's story, the Damned Thing's invisibility is not perfect. When it stands between a human observer and any distant object, the farther object is somehow blotted out of the observer's view. When the Damned Thing stands between an observer and a constellation in the night sky, that constellation is briefly eclipsed or blotted out. This blotting effect has the effect of rendering the Damned Thing visible, since we are able to detect its presence by seeing nothing at all where we ought to see something. And we know that O'Brien's ghoul does not have this same property of blotting out whatever exists behind it, since O'Brien's human narrator had ample time to view the creature and would have noticed this property if it were present.

So, Bierce's Damned Thing and O'Brien's ghoul are probably not the same species after all. Yet both of them are anomalies here on Earth. Can they perhaps have arrived here by the same route?

As I continued and deepened my readings into the

fictional world of Ambrose Bierce, I discovered one of his less well-known pieces, titled 'Science to the Front'. In this essay, Bierce introduces a fictional scientist who makes the following observation:

> ... in the visible world there are void places ... holes, as it were, through which animate and inanimate objects may fall into the invisible world ... Cavities exist in this other wise universal medium, as caverns exist in the earth, or cells in a Swiss cheese.

Bierce refers to these void places as *vacua*—the singular form would be *vacuole*—and he proposes that such *vacua* may be the explanation for reports in which human beings have allegedly vanished without a trace. (Ironically, Bierce himself eventually vanished without a trace in late 1913.) Here we have a possible answer to part of the riddle of O'Brien's invisible ghoul. Let us recall the account of O'Brien's narrator in describing how this creature attacked him: he was lying in bed, in the darkness, when abruptly this creature dropped upon him from a height. He did not hear the creature enter the room. Nor was there any object above his bed from which the ghoul could have dangled before it dropped upon him; if such an object were there, the narrator would have mentioned it. A gas-bracket would not support the weight of this creature as O'Brien's narrator describes it.

Until a more plausible explanation is offered, I propose the following: O'Brien's invisible ghoul is a native of some world other than our own, and it fell or plunged through a *vacuole* in its own world that terminated on Earth, in midair directly above the bed of O'Brien's human narrator. This explains how the anomalous ghoul came to be present in Manhattan, and it also explains how the ghoul was able to drop onto the narrator with no previous warning.

Ambrose Bierce's *vacua* might also explain how Bierce's Damned Thing came to be present in nineteenth-century rural America; it too came from some other world, but encountered a *vacuole* which brought it to our world.

I now had part of the answer to Fitz-James O'Brien's mystery, but some questions still remained. If the invisible ghoul came from another world, then what sort of world could that be? It would have to possess a gravity, air pressure, temperature and atmosphere similar to those of Earth, since the ghoul seemed to have no difficulty breathing in Earth's atmosphere and moving in Earth's gravity.

In the early 1980s, in a used-book shop in New York City, I discovered a remarkable novel for boys that was originally published in America in 1933: *The Land of No Shadow*, by Carl H. Claudy. I am surprised that this book and its author are not better known. Carl H. Claudy was an astonishing man: in 1898, he had been a prospector in the Klondike gold rush. He befriended the aviator Orville Wright, and in September 1908 Claudy was present to photograph the first-ever aircraft fatality. Throughout his adult life, Carl Claudy was active in the Freemasons.

The Land of No Shadow is the third of four science-fiction novels written by Claudy, published between 1933 and 1934 in a series titled *Adventures in the Unknown*. By chance, I encountered this novel before I was aware of the other three volumes in the series. I am thankful that I found this one first. All four novels in the *Adventures in the Unknown* series combine science fiction with horror, but *The Land of No Shadow* is by far the best-written and most frightening novel in the series. In fact, to this day, *The Land of No Shadow* is easily the single most frightening novel I have ever read.

The Land of No Shadow, written for boys, is the story of two young American college students named Ted Dolliver and Alan Kane. An elderly scientist at their college has invented a device that projects a dimensional gateway between our world and another planet which appears to occupy the same space as Earth yet in another dimension. After leaping through the gateway, Ted and Alan find themselves on a bizarre world of no colours and no shadows, containing only rock formations and a fresh-water ocean. There is light, but no visible sun in the overcast sky, and no discernible cycle of day and night. This Land of No Shadow appears to be inhabited by invisible humanoid creatures, but Ted and Alan are just occasionally able to glimpse fleeting details of their anatomies. After some extremely frightening adventures, Ted Dolliver manages to leap back through the interdimensional gateway and return to the scientist's laboratory. The fate of Alan Kane remains unknown at the end of this novel. The first time I finished reading *The Land of No Shadow*, I did not know that this matter was resolved in a further novel in the series, and I assumed that Alan Kane's fate would remain a perpetual mystery.

In the same way that I had wondered about the physiology of Fitz-James O'Brien's invisible ghoul, I wondered about the ecosystem and biome of Carl H.

Claudy's alien planet. Why did its ocean have fresh water rather than salt? Why was there light, yet no visible sun? Since the entire planet appears to consist of rock with no vegetation or lower life forms, then how did the invisible humanoids evolve? And how do they sustain themselves? If they eat, then what species do they feed upon? If they do not eat, how do they maintain their metabolisms?

I was able to determine some of the answers, thanks to discoveries in physics that were not known in Fitz-James O'Brien's nineteenth century nor in Carl Claudy's 1930s. Today we know that gravity is a force that can bend and distort time, and that physical space is warped and distorted by gravitational fields. I believe that the planet in Claudy's novel orbits the same star as our own Earth, but in a separate dimension of space. It is therefore captive in the sun's gravitational field, precisely like our own Earth. Out of all the tremendous quantity of energy radiating from our sun, a very small percentage leaks through the dimensional gap to illuminate the sky of that other planet, Claudy's Land of No Shadow.

In the early 1990s, after I had published a substantial number of short stories, I had an idea for a story that would eventually become my science-fiction novel *The Woman Between the Worlds*. In my original conception, this would be the story of a Victorian Englishman's encounter with an invisible woman: that is, an ordinary human female who has somehow contrived to turn herself invisible, like the protagonist in H.G. Wells's novel *The Invisible Man*. As I started to develop this idea into a full-length novel, I changed it. The invisible female would not be an Englishwoman after all, but rather she would be a humanoid alien whose invisibility would be her natural state. However, this change aroused other questions. If the she-alien is naturally invisible, then how would such an invisible life-form evolve and sustain itself? And what sort of world—what sort of ecosystem or biome—could create such a creature in the first place?

Then I remembered the invisible sentinels in Carl H. Claudy's novel *The Land of No Shadow*, and I decided that I would use Claudy's fictional planet as the scaffold on which I would construct my own fiction's alien world. But how would my invisible she-alien travel from her homeworld to Victorian London? Suddenly I remembered Ambrose Bierce's *vacua*, and I recalled Bierce's story 'The Damned Thing'. At the same time, I remembered Fitz-James O'Brien's story 'What Was It? A Mystery'. Now I had an audacious thought: I decided that my invisible she-alien, as well as O'Brien's invisible ghoul and Bierce's invisible Damned Thing, would *all be specimens of the same species*, originating on the same homeworld, and endowed with the same physical traits.

However, a novel must conform to rules that do not apply to a short story. O'Brien and Bierce could trot out their invisible monsters, achieve a shudder in the spine of the reader, then take a bow and exit without ever explaining their effects. I did not have that luxury. I would have to create plausible explanations for how my invisible creatures evolved and how they functioned.

To begin with, invisibility is a function of light. Air and water are both transparent, but a transparent raindrop is still visible in midair. This is because water is thicker than air, and therefore it has a different refractive index. The refractive index is a measure of the speed of light through a transparent medium; the more tangible or solid the medium, the greater the refractive index. A transparent ice cube is partially visible in clear water because most of the solid ice is thicker than the liquid water, and therefore has a different refractive index. The light-waves bend—or refract—when they pass from one medium to another. In order to be truly invisible in Earth's atmosphere, a life-form would have to possess the same refractive index as air ... but this can only occur if the life-form itself is as tenuous as air.

In the ecosystem of our own Earth, we have a few life-forms that are transparent in their natural state. Some of these are deep-sea creatures. One fascinating lifeform is the flowering plant known as Indian pipe (taxonomic name *Monotropa uniflora*). This forest plant does not contain chlorophyll. In its most natural state, the Indian pipe is completely transparent and is therefore difficult to notice against the forest floor. Unfortunately, due to modern pollution, the typical Indian pipe is now somewhat dingy in appearance, or even white as if it were albino. However, even a totally colourless Indian pipe is still visible to the careful observer, due to its refractive index in air.

A multicellular organism—or even a unicellular organism, such as a giant amoeba—would have to be substantially thicker than our planet's atmosphere. H.G. Wells hinted at this problem in his novel *The Invisible Man*, but did not resolve it. Basically, a transparent man standing in a transparent atmosphere would look like a giant bubble—a man-sized, man-shaped bubble—in midair, due to the different refractive indices of his body and the air surrounding him. The human body is basically a bag of water: in normal atmosphere, an invisible man would look like a clear bag of clear water, with a skeletal system resembling a transparent ice sculpture.

My novel is narrated by a Victorian Englishman, and nearly all the events of this novel are described from his viewpoint and through his senses. At several points in the novel, when my narrator is in the presence of the invisible woman or another member of her alien species, I describe him experiencing the sensation of perceiving some sort of *wrinkle* in the air in front of him, as if one portion of the atmosphere were somehow significantly thicker than the air surrounding it. In this manner, I dealt with the problem of an invisible humanoid's refractive index.

The creature in Fitz-James O'Brien's story is solid enough to be imprisoned by ropes securely tied. He—I am assuming that O'Brien's ghoul is *male*—is more solid than the air around him. Therefore he would appear as a transparent bubble, and the shape of the bubble would give some clue to the shape of O'Brien's creature. The same must be true of the Damned Thing in Bierce's tale.

Why did Bierce and O'Brien never mention this bubble-like appearance in their stories? In Bierce's case, where the invisible creature is observed outdoors in daylight, we have the blotting effect to explain why the Damned Thing is not totally invisible. In O'Brien's case, the creature in 'What Was It?' is observed only indoors, in a room illuminated by gaslight. Modern readers, accustomed to electricity, do not realise the extreme inferiority of coal-gas illumination. Gaslight was much dimmer than electrical light, and it constantly flickered due to impurities in the coal gas. I therefore maintain that

Fitz-James O'Brien's invisible ghoul was in fact quite visible after all—visible as a ghoul-shaped bubble in the room—but O'Brien's narrator and the other observers in his story either failed to notice this or failed to comment on it, due to the normal flickering and shifting of the light in a room illuminated by gas-brackets.

Next we have the problem of invisible eyes. An eye that is truly invisible is totally useless. If a human retina were to be rendered invisible—that is, if light were to pass through the retina of a human eye without being stopped or refracted—then that eye would be blind.

H. G. Wells was definitely aware of this. In his novel *The Invisible Man*, the title character first tests his invisibility process on a cat—successfully—before using it on himself. If you will read the text of Wells's novel very carefully, he makes very subtle but definite statements that the cat's eyes, and then the narrator's eyes, remain very faintly and nebulously visible after their bodies become transparent. Wells did not emphasise this faint visibility of his protagonist's eyes, because he did not want the other characters in his novel to have a means of seeing the Invisible Man.

What about Bierce's Damned Thing and Fitz-James O'Brien's ghoul? Both of them are predatory by nature, but we do not know for certain that either one of them is guided by sight. Snakes and bats are predatory species, but their eyes are almost totally useless ... and they find their prey by means of scent or, in the bat's case, scent combined with echolocation.

Let us assume, though, that Bierce's creature and O'Brien's creature do rely on their eyesight to the same extent that we humans do. How is it that these invisible creatures are not blind? One explanation is that perhaps their eyes are nebulously visible, but the narrators of their respective stories do not mention this. The Damned Thing didn't stand still long enough to be observed carefully. O'Brien's ghoul was observed at leisure, but only in a room illuminated by gaslight.

For *The Woman Between the Worlds*, I came up with another explanation. My novel's narrator absolutely establishes that the eyes of the aliens are as invisible as their flesh. It develops that the invisible aliens in my novel have eyes which perceive ultra-violet light, which to our own eyes is nearly always invisible. If one of my invisible creatures were placed underneath a U.V. lamp, not only its retinas and optic nerves but its entire body would become visible to a human observer.

However, eyes which have evolved for perceiving ultra-violet light will respond differently from human eyes. In my novel, the female alien tells the narrator that she is unable to see through a windowpane or any other sheet of glass. This is scientifically accurate: glass is opaque to ultra-violet light. Under a U.V. lamp, a sheet of clear glass appears black. What you and I perceive as total transparency, another species sees as utter blackness. Some humans have a superior ability to see ultra-violet radiation. People who undergo surgery to remove cataracts from their eyes often experience a greater ability to see light in U.V. wavelengths than before they developed cataracts.

I concede the possibility that Fitz-James O'Brien's monster, or Ambrose Bierce's Damned Thing, or both, may have evolved with eyes that see ultra-violet light rather than our own familiar colours. If this is the case, they would have no difficulty finding their prey here on Earth. A large amount of the sun's radiation is in the U.V. portion of the spectrum, and coal gas also emits some of its energy in the ultra-violet wavelengths. Let us recall that Fitz-James O'Brien's creature first attacks the narrator in a room that is totally dark, or at least dark to human eyes. Either O'Brien's creature has access to some other form of illumination that we cannot see, or else—like a bat or a snake—it is capable of finding its prey without eyesight at all.

My mention of "prey" raises the question of how an invisible life-form sustains itself. Fitz-James O'Brien's creature is so very humanoid—so similar to a human in so many respects—that I make a reasonable assumption that the creature stays alive the same way that we do, by eating and excreting. In the story of Ambrose Bierce's Damned Thing, we know that the creature eats human flesh as well as lower animals. In Fitz-James O'Brien's story, after the invisible creature has been securely bound, the narrator observes:

> We were entirely ignorant of what the creature habitually fed on. Everything in the way of nutriment that we could think of was placed before it, but was never touched.

The narrator does not offer any details, but I suspect that there was a flaw in his methods, due to the sensitivities in his Victorian breeding; namely, every food that was offered to O'Brien's creature was already dead. Although many species feed on carrion, there are other species that prefer live food ... again, snakes and bats devour their prey while it is still alive, and then kill it through the digestive process.

In *The Woman Between the Worlds*, I make clear that my invisible aliens are perfectly willing to eat a living man. Actually, an entire man contains more meat than one of the aliens can comfortably digest in a single meal, but my point is that the live flesh will sustain their digestive systems. Fitz-James O'Brien's narrator was in bed, half-asleep and quite innocent when the invisible creature attacked him ... I believe that the creature attacked him with the intention of eating him, or at least eating part of him. If the humans in O'Brien's story had offered their captive a live chicken, or any living small animal such as a cat, I believe that the invisible monster would have eaten it.

O'Brien's narrative mentions the body heat of the creature. It is therefore a mammal, or at least is similar to a mammal in possessing an internal heat source to regulate its body temperature. Here, the invisible ghoul is unlike a snake but still similar to a bat, which is a predatory mammal. A distinctive feature of mammals is that predatory species such as dogs and cats have their eyes on the front of their heads, while non-predatory mammals such as mice and rabbits have their eyes on the sides. They have evolved these traits so that predators can better pursue their prey and non-predators can more easily see the predators approaching. We humans have our eyes on the front of our heads because we are predators. Fitz-James O'Brien's narrator gives only a cursory description of his invisible creature's face, but describes it as similar to a human's. If it had deviated from a human by having its eyes placed laterally rather than forward, O'Brien's narrator would surely have mentioned such a significantly non-human characteristic.

In view of all the above, I absolutely maintain that O'Brien's invisible creature was a carnivorous predator, probably accustomed to eating live prey. Thus far, it is identical in every particular to the invisible alien species in my own novel.

Now there arises the question of ingestion, digestion and egestion: how does an invisible life-form eat, and what happens to the food afterwards? Hollywood has not always been logical in answering this question. Thus, in the movie *Abbott and Costello Meet the Invisible Man*, we have an invisible man swallowing long strands of spaghetti. The spaghetti is perfectly visible as it rises towards his invisible mouth, but as soon as the spaghetti enters his mouth it immediately vanishes in midair, as if some instantaneous chemical reaction has occurred.

H. G. Wells was aware of this problem. In his novel, a doctor named Kemp is able to see what the Invisible Man has recently eaten as a ghostly image in midair, inside the Invisible Man's transparent stomach. The Invisible Man acknowledges that he must remain hidden for an hour or so after he has eaten, while his lunch becomes as invisible as the rest of him. Evidently, the digestive enzymes in his body have some ability to break down his food in such a manner that it becomes transparent within his invisible body. This is possible, in the sense that anything an invisible man eats will gradually become part of the invisible man.

My novel contains a scene in which the invisible she-alien eats meat while the human narrator watches.

When her invisible teeth chew the meat, he has the impression of seeing the food tear itself to shreds in midair. After the alien has eaten, the food remains faintly visible within her invisible body until she digests it.

What about excretion? I am amused by the notion of watching an invisible man urinate. We would see a bubble of liquid in midair, corresponding to the size and shape of a human bladder. Suddenly, the urine escapes with great speed, in a trajectory corresponding to the the invisible man's other toilet functions, but the same principle applies in the colon and intestines.

Fitz-James O'Brien's narrator keeps his invisible creature captive for many weeks, yet never mentions the creature urinating or defecating. There are several possible explanations for this. The simplest explanation is that the creature had normal functions of urination and excretion, but O'Brien's Victorian sensibilities prevented him from offending his readers by mentioning this. Indeed, H.G. Wells—writing four decades later but still in the Victorian era—makes no mention of what happens or what it looks like when his Invisible Man goes to the loo.

I prefer another explanation. Here on Earth, the marsupial mammals have a urinary system completely different from that of placental mammals: a system which allows them to concentrate their urine and delay dehydration, urinating less frequently than placental mammals. O'Brien's invisible creature is held captive for weeks without ingesting either food or water. In all that time, it apparently has no need to excrete solid or liquid wastes. My explanation is as follows: much as we humans make a trip to the lavatory before embarking

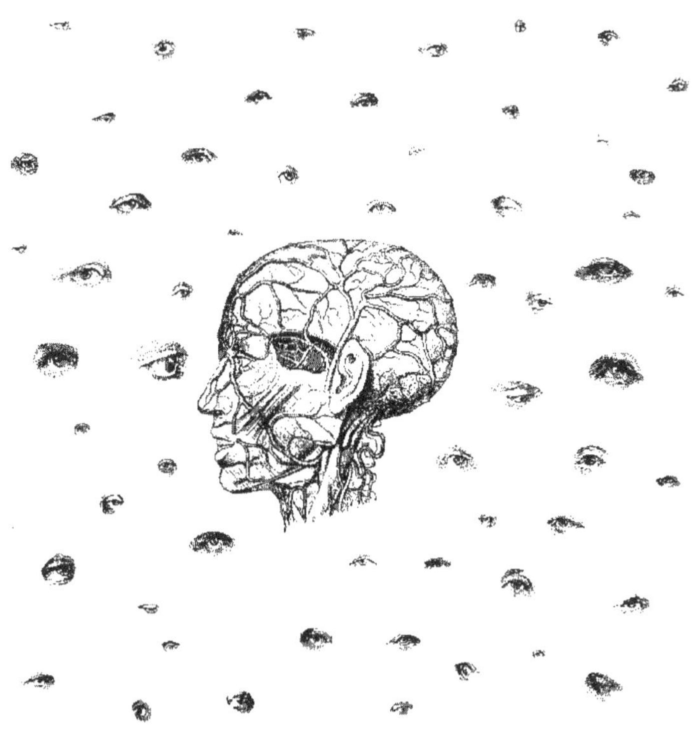

An illustration from *The Woman Between the Worlds*

on a long trip, O'Brien's invisible creature must have made ablutions on its homeworld before plunging into the *vacuole* which brought it to New York City ... and, once captured, because it did not ingest any nutrients for several weeks, it had no need to excrete waste products.

Now let us consider what sort of planet and ecosystem would enable such a creature to evolve into existence. When I decided that the invisible aliens in *The Woman Between the Worlds* would be based on the same species as O'Brien's invisible ghoul, I also decided that their home planet would be based on the Land of No Shadow in Carl Claudy's novel of that name. I named that planet Kavnoklor; this being the alien people's name for their homeworld in their own language.

Claudy's novel *The Land of No Shadow* is a masterpiece of understatement, because it gives only the barest details of the trans-dimensional world into which his human protagonists are flung. It is a world of perpetual twilight, containing stone and air and ocean; nothing more, except for the faces and bodies of inhuman observers that are just barely visible for brief intervals. The air is breathable to the human visitors, with no ill effects. There are no discernible rivers nor lakes, but the oceans have water which the humans are able to drink safely, although this water is slightly brackish.

I transferred those traits to the alien planet in my novel, and gave an explanation: the alien planet Kavnoklor rotates on its axis much more slowly than our Earth, and lacks any satellite corresponding to our own moon. Therefore Kavnoklor has no tides, and the oceans have not become salted with minerals eroded from the land mass.

However, at this point I found it necessary to depart from Claudy's text. My invisible creatures are carnivores; therefore, they must have evolved within an ecosystem along with lower species that would serve as their prey. I did not want to dilute the plot of my novel with an entire taxonomy for the planet Kavnoklor, but I briefly mentioned a weird flapping white creature that propels itself across the surface of the ocean, and which is able to come up onto the shore. My conception of this creature was inspired by the superb ghost stories of the Victorian author M.R. James. Throughout James's work, there is a continuous motif in which the colour *white* is associated with horror, and his supernatural creatures have a tendency to flap and convulse.

I did not describe my white flapping creatures in detail, but mentioned them only to establish within my novel that the invisible ghouls of Kavnoklor are not the only life-form native to their planet, and that an entire ecosystem or biome is in place.

I also made one change to the landscape of my planet that was not present in Claudy's novel. In both novels, the continental land mass consists of a single vast plateau, separated from the ocean by sheer cliffs which appear to have no foothills. I decided to add enormous boulders, almost perfectly spherical, to the nightscape of my world Kavnoklor. I never explain what process of erosion would create such giant boulders and shape them to such perfect roundness. However, in Claudy's novel *The Land of No Shadow*, the invisible aliens are able to drill deep cylindrical pits into the bedrock of their planet ... apparently by sheer force of will, without any drilling equipment or other technology.

In the early stages of writing *The Woman Between the Worlds*, I was absolutely determined to keep the invisible humanoids in my novel the same species as Fitz-James O'Brien's invisible ghoul. Both stories are told in first-person narration by a young male observer. In fact, I had originally planned to use the last sentence of O'Brien's story 'What Was It?' as the closing sentence in my own novel, as follows:

> As I am on the eve of a long journey from which I may not return, I have drawn up the narrative of an event the most singular that has ever come to my knowledge.

Because my novel is much longer and more detailed than Fitz-James O'Brien's brief story, it became clear to me that I would eventually have to reward my readers with a specific explanation of the invisible creatures' physical structure and physiognomy. I looked for clues in O'Brien's story. His creature is described as possessing body heat, respiration and a heartbeat. Since O'Brien's invisible ghoul did not asphyxiate on Earth, it must therefore be able to breathe our planet's air without ill effects.

In *The Woman Between the Worlds*, I wrote a scene in which the Englishman narrator is alone on the seafront in the coastal town of Weston-super-Mare on Christmas Eve. Snow has fallen, and the December air is so cold that his breath condenses into a fog of visible vapour as he exhales. Suddenly, he sees a series of footprints forming in the snow, moving towards him ... prints more resembling a trail of cloven hoofprints rather than human feet. One of the invisible aliens confronts him, alone on the seafront. As they speak, the human narrator discovers that he can see the internal body cavity of his invisible enemy as an outline, because the carbon dioxide in the creature's invisible lungs is condensing in the cold, to form a perceptible vapour. He can also make out some details of the invisible creature's face, as its visible breath escapes from its unseen mouth and nose.

Eventually, the invisible she-alien is abducted back to her home planet Kavnoklor, and her Englishman friend must plunge through the same dimensional gateway to rescue her, accompanied by the bizarre Victorian eccentric Aleister Crowley. It develops in my novel that Crowley, unlike most humans, has the ability to see a portion of the ultra-violet spectrum. Therefore the invisible aliens are faintly visible to him.

Early in *The Woman Between the Worlds*, there is a sequence in which the Englishman narrator locates a vein in the invisible she-alien's arm, and he injects her with a bright red dye. He then proceeds to watch in astonishment as the dye spreads through her circulatory system, gradually revealing her invisible body's contours. Although she is approximately human in size and shape, she has two hearts. In 'What Was It?', a doctor is summoned to chloroform the invisible creature. The narrator had no way of knowing in advance that chloroform would affect this creature's respiratory system in the same way that it affects a human; nevertheless, this is the case. O'Brien's narrator states that the creature has a heartbeat. So far, I have designed my invisible alien species to be consistent with O'Brien's invisible creature. They both have body heat, they both have circulatory systems. Since I have endowed my invisible aliens with a double heart, I now maintain for the record that O'Brien's

"What Was It?" creature likewise possesses two hearts. But those hearts beat simultaneously rather than alternatively; therefore, O'Brien's narrator only observed a single heartbeat.

At about the midpoint in my novel, in a scene on the alien world Kavnoklor, I felt that it was time at last to describe in detail what these invisible aliens actually look like. Once again, I consulted Fitz-James O'Brien's story. His narrator states that his invisible ghoul has a face resembling one of the illustrations in Tony Johannot's novel *A Voyage to Where You Please*. I consulted that novel. I also consulted Carl Claudy's *The Land of No Shadow*, in which his two human protagonists are able to snatch brief glimpses of their invisible captors. In Claudy's novel, the invisible aliens in his Land of No Shadow are just barely visible when glimpsed peripherally, from the edge of the observer's field of vision. When looked at directly, they vanish. Here is Claudy's most detailed description of his invisible sentinels:

> A quarter of a mile away, two faces stood out of the mist; faces that changed as the adventurers looked at them! The mouths were lipless, and as Ted and Alan watched they disappeared. Beneath the faces a dim suggestion of bodies—huge and barrel-like—took momentary form,and then faded.

I had difficulty reconciling this description with Bierce's Damned Thing, or Fitz-James O'Brien's ghoul, or my own denizens of Kavnoklor. Claudy's aliens are so large that their faces can be seen from a quarter of a mile away, and they also possess the ability to move through solid rock. Claudy suggests that his creatures exist within a fourth dimension of space, and therefore they are invisible to us because we can only glimpse the portions of them which fleetingly pass through our own three dimensions. I did not want to make my aliens fourth-dimensional. However, Claudy's use of the word "barrel-like" led me to visualise O'Brien's ghoul as barrel-chested. After revisiting all three sources—O'Brien's story, Claudy's novel, and Tony Johannot's illustrations (which O'Brien had cited) —I developed the anatomy for my own invisible aliens, borrowing something from each. Here is how they look when my Victorian narrator is finally able to see them:

> The things were shaped like parodies of men. Twisted, deformed; a thousand hunchbacks on parade. Their arms and their legs and their barrel-shaped chests revealed a muscular development astonishing in its prodigy. Their fingers and toes were long and thin, and appeared to be prehensile. Their genitals were as distorted and over-sized as the priapic appendage of some pagan sex-god. They had no necks worth mentioning, and their chins dangled down against the swellings of their ribs. Their noses were broadened and flattened, and in several cases the face was so sharp and elongated as to take the appearance of a snout. The lips of these creatures were thickened, slavering, and their teeth jutted out of their grin-slitted mouths like so many fangs. The eyes, I think, were most hideous of all: they bulged alarmingly as though ready to burst from their sockets, and the irises and pupils had narrowed to a pinpoint in the centre of each eye. The fiends looked capable of feasting on human flesh.

All of the above is compatible with what we know of the creature in Fitz-James O'Brien's story. The description of my creatures could apply to O'Brien's as well. I have added one further dimension by establishing that my creatures are a two-sexed species, with some individuals being male and others being female.

Now that I have built this elaborate house of cards, constructing an entire ecosystem and physiology to link my own invisible creatures to the species conceived by Fitz-James O'Brien, it is time for me to demolish what I have built. In *The Woman Between the Worlds*, I decided to make my aliens *shape-changers*, as well as invisible. However, I did not want them to possess the protean abilities of an amoeba, able to morph itself into any shape at all like the Changeling character Odo in *Star Trek: Deep Space Nine*. My invisible aliens are able to attenuate their limbs to an extreme length, and able to alter the contours of their faces and bodies, but only within a limit slightly beyond the ability of humans. I have mentioned one invisible alien leaving hoofprints in the snow, rather than footprints: he altered the structures of his feet into appendages that are better suited than human feet for walking on snow. On solid ground, his hooves would morph into humanoid feet once again.

However, I must confront the fact that this shape-shifting ability, which is very limited and has only minor importance in my novel, serves as conclusive proof that my invisible aliens are not the same species as O'Brien's creature after all. If O'Brien's ghoul was a shape-shifter, it would have been impossible for his human captors to restrain him by tying him up: he would simply have narrowed himself and escaped his bondage. Yet we know that the creature's human captors were indeed able to render him captive ... to the point where he was unable to escape, and eventually starved to death.

So, in the final reckoning, all the traits which I have

applied to my own invisible aliens do not apply to O'Brien's creature after all, except by coincidence. There is precisely one literary work that can definitely be linked to Fitz-James O'Brien's 'What Was It?' ... and that is his own previous story, 'A Pot of Tulips'. Both stories are narrated by a man named Harry Escott, and in 'What Was It?' the narrator definitely states that he is the author of the previous story.

Since O'Brien's story 'A Pot of Tulips' is less frequently printed and more obscure than his story 'What Was It?', I shall mention that 'A Pot of Tulips' is a ghost story in which Harry Escott unites a young heiress named Alice with her lost fortune, and he then proceeds to marry her. However, in the sequel 'What Was It? A Mystery', no mention is made of this maiden. Harry Escott is once again a bachelor ... although evidently a bachelor with an independent income. Pray tell, then: what happened to Alice? Perhaps our Harry murdered her ... and the invisible creature that lands on his chest in the middle of the night is the tangible incarnation of his conscience.

If that is the case, then O'Brien's narrator is a man who allowed his own conscience to slowly starve to death.

Five Poems

Rethabile Masilo

Mordad

~for Ordibehesht

The face of your father comes
through flung windows into the bedroom
of this sweltering August. In a bid
to keep us from needing the dead,
he floats toward the bed where the four of us
lie sprawled, helpless in this heat.
I indulge in the vision of my father-in-law
holding my hand the night of his visit.
Overcome by decades and hapless days,
the face of your father comes when I'm awake
as when I'm asleep. I wear it like a mask,
penetrate a different peace
where no one's allowed to weep.
They come out every night for a spell
to touch the world, he says, they leave behind
gravestone, garlands, wilting plants,
and long to be with us a while.

Midwinter

Think of a doorway
in some *vieux quartier*
where we would live, think
of it in your own breath,
not of the face whose body
the ice caps, then when
something snaps, is it
the sound of a bone,
or is it a prey-like shriek
at night when the moon
cowers behind a cloud
and a loose shutter battles
its window? You will know
that whoever this is
is you in a different case,
under different circumstances,
and you're not going to return,
but will accept the fact
to expect no Samaritan,

in the doorway where you live
even as the croak of your voice
rises to reach the clothes
of the next person scurrying to work
or back, they will not listen,
curtains will be withdrawn
and quickly drawn again.
You will think, 'What a relief
that no one has to haul me
to their flat in front of curious
neighbours.' This you will begin
to acknowledge, and will say
to the world and to yourself,
'What a drag that would have been.'

Echoes

We are hollow inside,
everything of us
is pipes instead of guts.
No bells ring on the morning
of our sky.
The priest is hollow
in his robes, gold clings
to him from the bottom
of his hem to the top,
the heads of politicians are hollow,
ostrich eggs abandoned in the desert.
You're hollow, for all is.
Scour with your hand now
cream from the two-day old
milk bowl and stuff it
down your hole.

Seven

In the morning, when it's seven,
sunrise leads us down the stone slope
of our childhood to the river, for water.
Above us the precipice of Qoaling,
where we live, juts like a forehead
over the valley and sends fingers
to map out the terrain with erosion;
still, fruit here drops with the weight
of a heart tired out from fighting
the government. One day a spirit
entered me and sat on my heart
with its face of darkness, my arms
crushed under it like dry branches.
That day I died for seven minutes,
and got to this place called heaven
where they take you in, if the sun
has quit giving you the rest of life.
To me, listening to the sound of stars
up there, sitting inside a symphony
of sitars, only meant that I was dead.

Six days later the world and its light,
the sun's irreducible heat, plus one
day set aside to while away time,
these had already been put in place
as I turned back and headed home,
the wonders of a world that Egypt
ruled, as many wonders as any land
could stand, the will to erect things,
built from the ground up; to this day
seven monuments including Babel,
as well as Babylon's famous gardens
which hang from walls like perfumed
hair, as if seven, counted first as five
on one hand, then two on the other,
were the only number that chance
could give the lucky, as if each stone
the builder touches becomes alive.

The Cycle

Watching the sky
on a day in autumn,
I saw light fill gaps
in the forest.
A hand crept from the earth,
grabbed our shins
and said death was on us,
so we laid low on the yellow bed
and played dead, believing
its grip of cold fingers
that we too must die
in order to live,
the cycle of life,
of giving body away
in a never-ending sequence
of seasonal change,
the rise, the fall of it all.

An Inquiry
into the Narrator's Psychological Conundrum in O'Brien's 'What Was It? A Mystery'

Cécile Chartier

Fitz-James O'Brien's short story 'What Was It? A Mystery' conspicuously revolves around an invisible creature's definition—or lack thereof. We first encounter it in a nightly visitation to a New York mansion, struggling with the narrator, Harry Escott. Its nature and *raison d'être* seems to be the heart of the matter, its name a mystery, its mere existence a challenge to the inhabitants' 19th century rational—yet surprisingly superstitious—minds. All the characters are focused on examining, questioning, wondering at that creature. It is given many appellations: "a Something", "the Enigma", and "the Mystery" to name but a few. Critics, too, link the true meaning of the story to the nature of the invisible creature: a symbol of the fantastic genre for some,[1] the representation of the starving Irish people for others,[2] a threat to white male superiority for others still.[3] Its very blankness allows readers to project their own interpretative desires.

Yet, in the midst of this interpretative *mêlée*, one character evades the scrutiny it deserves, and for a very good reason: Harry Escott, the narrator, repeatedly points to the creature as both the blind spot and the focal point of the story. As obedient readers, we tend to follow his paradoxical injunction to scrutinize the inscrutable. But what if the true meaning of the story lay in its telling? Why not thoroughly question the reliability of the narrator?

The narrator's insistent affirmation of his own authority is suspicious from the start. The opening lines intertwine a legitimate narrative caveat with bold self-conceit:

> It is, I confess, with considerable diffidence that I approach the strange narrative which I am about to relate. The events which I purpose detailing are of so extraordinary and unheard-of a character that I am quite prepared to meet with an unusual amount of incredulity and scorn. I accept all such beforehand. I have, I trust, the literary courage to face unbelief. I have, after mature consideration, resolved to narrate, in as simple and straightforward a manner as I can compass, some facts that passed under my observation in the month of July last, and which, in the annals of the mysteries of physical science, are wholly unparalleled.[4]

Although laden with verbal hedge and apparent self-effacement, and mocking Indian Chief George W. Harkins' 'Letter to the American People',[5] the beginning of the story is in reality the beginning of a long self-promotional endeavor. First of all, his claim of literary "courage" and authority seems to be the corner stone of his enterprise. It is further substantiated by his later admittance of having authored a previous supernatural story, 'The Pot of Tulips', in the same literary paper, *Harper's New Monthly Magazine*. It has to be noted that the name of the paper, as well as that of the narrator and other narrative characteristics of this magazine story were edited out by William Winter in his authoritative collection of O'Brien's poems and short stories in 1881, so all of the intertextual and self-reflexive dimension has passed mostly unnoticed until now.

But this literary feat, which seems to have unwittingly "leaked out" to his fellow boarders and given him much credit among them, poses at the same time interesting questions as to the status of the text, thus undermining the credit that we, readers, give the text. 'The Pot of Tulips' was first presented as a true testimony. If it was actually fiction, how can we not doubt the authenticity of 'What Was It?' as a true testimony?

Another Winter-edited detail raises questions as to the narrator's literary authority: when evoking the opium-induced literary conversation he would have with his sidekick Dr Hammond, Escott writes "If we talked of Shakespeare's 'Midsummer Night's Dream,' we lingered over Ariel and avoided Caliban." For someone who boasts about his literary capacities, the confusion between *A Midsummer Night's Dream* and *The Tempest* is nothing short of outrageous. William Winter may have attributed this *lapsus calami* to O'Brien himself (thus maybe betraying how poorly he truly considered O'Brien as a writer), but it is far more meaningful to assign it to Harry Escott and see him as something of a literary con man—either not a very good one, or one who scatters clues for his enlightened readers.

Apart from asserting some literary superiority—over his fellow boarders, even over Dr Hammond—Escott also considers himself to be a matchless scientific mind. After all, the opening lines do inform us that he aims at nothing less than revolutionizing physical science by his discovery. He conducts his adventure as scientific experiment: "[I] felt a sort of scientific pride in the affair which dominated every other feeling".[6] More importantly, any claim that he might be the victim of his opium consumption is rebutted on account of his scientific power:

> Those hours of opium happiness which the doctor and I spent together in secret were regulated by a scientific accuracy. We did not blindly smoke the drug of Paradise, and leave our dreams to chance.[7]

Instead of being a slave to opium, Escott is its master, and affirms he is capable of steering through the rough seas of elation unharmed thanks to his mental power.

In this respect, the story can be read in the light of some of Edgar Allan Poe's stories. Of course, 'What Was It?' cannot be mistaken for a story by Poe: there is no barely visible or audible presence, no progression of terror by slow degrees, no obvious sign of the narrator's mental imbalance, no over-acuteness of senses. However, O'Brien plants subtle hints about his predecessor: the initial reference to a previous story makes it comparable to 'The Purloined Letter', and, of course, the title itself is an utterly Poesque question.[8] But most of all, the eagerness of the narrator to present himself as the paragon of rationality should draw our attention. Does it not echo strangely the claims made by the narrator of 'The Tell-Tale Heart'?

> Now this is the point. You fancy me mad. Madmen know nothing. But you should have seen me. You should have seen how wisely I proceeded—with what caution—with what foresight—with what dissimulation I went to work![9]

But while 'The Tell-Tale Heart's narrator only attracts attention to his madness by denying it, Harry Escott develops strategies to maintain the appearance of absolute sanity.

The first strategy is to have a partner, another character who serves for the reasoning to progress through dialogue. This was introduced by Poe with his ratiocinating two-person team made up of C. Auguste Dupin and the anonymous narrator[10]. The questions and answers allow for the mental process to be expressed verbally. Specifically in 'What Was It?', the presence of another character appears to be a guarantee that the creature is not just a figment of Escott's imagination: it is "scientifically proven" by Dr Hammond. It also gives Escott the opportunity to answer the reader's doubts:

> "Harry," whispered Hammond approaching me, "you have been smoking too much opium." [...] Hammond advanced and laid his hand in the spot I indicated. A wild cry of horror burst from him. He had felt it![11]

But Dr Hammond is more to Escott than the anonymous narrator is to Dupin:

> Independent of certain mental sympathies which existed between the Doctor and myself, we were linked together by a secret vice. We smoked opium. We knew each other's secret, and respected it. We enjoyed together that wonderful expansion of thought. [...] Our pleasures,while individual, were still twin, vibrating and moving in musical accord.[12]

Now the whole the point of the partnership Dupin/the anonymous narrator is Dupin's intellectual superiority, as witnessed by the narrator and with some effects of concealing information or delaying its full disclosure—the same is true of Arthur Conan Doyle's Sherlock Holmes and Dr Watson.[13] But here the proximity between both characters, their "opium brotherhood", so to speak, and the equality of their reasoning faculties, make them doubles more than anything else. Hammond is a duplicate of Escott, giving his words twice as much credit.

Not only has the narrator a double in the character of Dr Hammond, it also has a negative counterpart: the creature itself. Indeed the descriptions of the creature are characterized by the recurring use of negative affixes: "invisible", of course, but also "unseen", "irregular", "impotently", "unusual", "impossible", "inanimate", "uncouth", "unearthly being", "unparalleled" and "viewless" are some instances. Grammatical negations pile up: "not unaccountable" (repeated twice), "not theoretically impossible", "[they] did not dare to undeceive themselves". Defining by negating is the narrator's recurring strategy, as he confines the creature to nothingness. Self-promotion is correlated with the creature's demotion to the status of a thing, an undefinable object, a freak of nature. Besides, stressing the creature's invisibility makes one detail pass unnoticed: its total muteness. In the end the creature is subjugated because of the narrator's physical strength but also, and perhaps more importantly, because of his elocutionary superiority. Escott's narrative power is reflected by the creature's narrative subjection.
The true mystery resides in the narrator, of whom the creature is but a negative reflection. The creature is here to reveal the monstrosity of the narrator, who rejects responsibility and passes guilt over to that invisible and mute creature, like a child would to his

imaginary friend or a psychopath to another persona of his psyche. The story starts by a liminal conversation about pure terror, and the *peripeteia* comes as an illustration of it. In fact, what is truly terrifying for the narrator is the possibility that the true identity of "it" is "I".

Notes

1 Steven Dimeo, 'Psychological Symbolism in Three Early Tales of Invisibility', *Riverside Quarterly 5*, MLA-IB, 1971, pp.20–27.

2 Charles Fanning, *The Irish Voice in America: 250 Years of Irish-American Fiction*, (2nd ed.). Kentucky: The University Press of Kentucky, 2000.

3 Joyce L. Huff, 'The Domesticated Monster: Freakishness and Masculinity in Fitz-James O'Brien's 'What Was It?", *Nineteenth-Century Gender Studies 4*, no. 2, 2008, http://www.ncgsjournal.com/issue42/huff.htm. Retreived 30 November, 2013

4 'What Was It?', p.3.

5 The genuinely humble as well as highly pertinent letter starts thus: "It is with considerable diffidence that I attempt to address the American people, knowing and feeling sensibly my incompetency; and believing that your highly and well improved minds would not be well entertained by the address of a Choctaw. But having determined to emigrate west of the Mississippi river this fall, I have thought proper in bidding you farewell to make a few remarks expressive of my views, and the feelings that actuate me on the subject of our removal." Harkins George W., 'George W. Harkins to the American People - December 1831', http://ualr.edu/sequoyah/index.php/george-w-harkins-to-the-american-people-december-1831/. Retrieved 13 April, 2012.

6 'What Was It?', p.16.

7 *Ibid.*, p.7.

8 "I had done a deed—what was it? I asked myself the question aloud, and the whispering echoes of the chamber answered me,—'What Was It?'" 'Berenicë', Edgar Allan Poe, *Selected Tales*. Oxford: Oxford World's Classics, 1998, p.19; "The expression of the eyes of Ligeia! How for long hours have I pondered upon it! How have I, through the whole of a midsummer night, struggled to fathom it! What was it—that something more profound that the well of Democritus—which lay far within the pupils of my beloved? What was it? I was possessed with a passion to discover." 'Ligeia', p.28; "What was it—I paused to think—what was it that so unnerved me in the contemplation of the House of Usher? It was a mystery all insoluble; nor could I grapple with the shadowy fancies that crowded upon me as I pondered." 'The Fall of the House of Usher', p.49.

9 'The Tell-Tale Heart', *Op. Cit.,* p.193.

10 There is a reference to Poe's ratiocination stories in Escott's previous story, 'The Pot or Tulips', talking about Escott's then-partner Jasper Joyce: "Jasper, if ever I am Emperor of France, I will make you chief of police; your inductive reasonning is magnificent." 'The Pot of Tulips', *Harper's New Monthly Magazine*, November 1855, p.813.

11 'What Was It?', p.14.

12 *Ibid.*, pp.7-8.

13 For more insight on the place of O'Brien's stories in the tradition of the detective story, see Pete Orford, 'What are they? The Pseudo-mystery stories of Fitz-James O'Brien', *Clues: A Journal of Detection*, 30:2, Autumn 2012, pp.10–18.

Invisibility in 'What Was It? A Mystery'

Folie écrite ou folie vécue?

Alexandra Tauvry

The italicized part of my title is taken from the preface to 'Le Horla' written by Guy de Maupassant in 1887. This 19th-century French writer wrote prolifically on supernatural themes in the same vein as his less famous predecessor, Fitz-James O'Brien. Although O'Brien did not achieve the literary reputation he deserved in his lifetime, he is remembered as a prominent figure of New York City's bohemian set and is now regarded as the heir of Edgar Allan Poe and a precursor of modern science fiction. By the time 'What was it? A Mystery' was published in March 1859 in *Harper's New Monthly Magazine*, he had already published one of his most accomplished short stories, 'The Diamond Lens'. Despite his short-lived career, he introduced the notion of invisibility into the literary field and inspired many writers in the decades following his death.

In 'What Was It?', O'Brien's narrator reports an event which occured in a house in New York, at the heart of which is an invisible creature. On first reading this story, we may find ourselves at a bit of a loss as the key question—what was it?—remains unanswered.[1] The only source of information is the narrator, Harry Escott, who is directly implicated in the events described.[2] We may, therefore, question the reliability of this narrator as Cécile Chartier does in the essay included in this volume. How does the narrator relate to the invisible creature? What does this incorporeal being represent? Is this a pure literary fiction or is there something more to it? The point of my study is to try to understand the nature of this invisible creature in the light of other 19th-century supernatural stories which all question the position of the narrator *vis-à-vis* an invisible being or an evil "other".

Returning to Maupassant, we discover that there are many points of resemblance between 'Le Horla' and 'What Was It?'. In the first version of 'Le Horla', the sick man says that he was resting in a room on July 20 and that, on the table, a book by Alfred de Musset was open at the poem 'La nuit de mai'. In O'Brien's story, the narrator moves to the new house in the month of May and narrates a supernatural encounter which occured in the month of July. Both stories revolve around a mystery: Maupassant's narrator exclaims "comme il est profond, ce *mystère* de l'Invisible!"[3] and the story he narrates similarly revolves around the *thing* that haunts him and the difficulty he has in *identifying* it. Notwithstanding the mysteriousness of the creature, the narrator of the French story manages to put a name on it, even if the name itself describes rather than solves the mystery. The neologism "horla" may derive from the vernacular word *horsain* meaning "a stranger" in Maupassant's native Normandy:

> Ce Horla, qui est-ce? Le passant surnaturel de Maupassant lui-même? Son double? Son vampire, comme disait Baudelaire, ou son surmoi, comme l'on nous dit que nous en avons tous un, plus ou moins maléfique, homicide et castrateur, mais toujours présent?[4]

In this excerpt from the preface to 'Le Horla', André Fermigier makes a few highly insightful remarks about this "horla" which are also relevant in the case of 'What was it?'. Could this invisible being be Maupassant himself? The French writer was confronted with madness in his family circle and was apparently inclined to it himself, which was not the case of O'Brien. Nonetheless, it is tempting to identify the invisible creature in 'What Was It?' with the narrator, Harry Escott. In fact, the latter describes the invisible thing as having a throat as fleshy and a skin as smooth as his own, thereby suggesting a connection between the two of them. This is how he narrates the course of the night's events:

> I resolved to go to sleep at once; so turning down my gas until nothing but a little *blue* point of light glimmered on the top of the tube, I composed to rest once more. The room was in total darkness. The atom of gas that still remained lighted did not illuminate a distance of three inches round the burner. I desperately drew my arm across my eyes, as if to shut out even the darkness, and tried to think of nothing. It was in vain. The confounded themes touched on by Hammond in the garden kept obtruding themselves on my brain. I battled against them.[5]

In this soliloquy, Escott is assailed by vile thoughts that are reminiscent of those harassing the soon-to-be deposed monarch in William Shakespeare's play, *Richard III*:

> The lights burn *blue*. It is now dead midnight. Cold fearful drops stand on my trembling flesh.What do I fear? Myself? There's no one else by.[6]

O'Brien's narrator is similarly plunged into an abyss of

tormenting inner thoughts, thereby suggesting that this evil may well be a part of himself. Alternatively, this invisible creature could embody the narrator's *double*.

In 'What Was it? A Mystery', the narrator subtly refers to the scientific research of the time by saying that the events which befall him "in the annals of the mysteries of physical science, are wholly unparalleled."[7] The short stories of Maupassant and O'Brien are separated by a period of almost thirty years, during which scientific progress had shed new light on certain enigmatic phenomena. The development of psychology and the notion of the subconscious was the talk of the day shortly after 'Le Horla' was published. Arguably, the theme of the "other self" that is always present in every one of us lurks just below the surface of 'What Was It?'.

With this in mind, we can read into Harry Escott's nickname for the boarding house—the abode of spirits—an anticipation of W. B. Yeats's *Spiritus Mundi*. Expounded in *A Vision* (1925), this is a vast reservoir from which images appear, every one of which corresponds to the antiself of a human being. To Yeats, this "Daemon" is the direct opposite of the self. The "black afreets" erupting from the depths of both Escott's and Hammond's talk, may well be versions of this other being, of our antithetical self, since an "afreet" is an evil demon or monster.[8] Furthermore, Hammond mentions the existence of "spirit circles" where people were overpowered by strange evil beings who seized control of their actions. The motif of the "antiself" or "double" is the main theme of a number of stories published around the same time as O'Brien's.

This "evil twin" also pervades Fyodor Dostoevsky's novella *The Double: A Petersburg Poem* published in 1846, almost ten years before 'What Was It?'. O'Brien had acquired very cosmopolitan tastes and, despite the fact that there was no English translation of this book in his lifetime, it is possible that he was familiar with the narrative of Yakov Petrovich Golyadkin and his internal psychological struggle.[9]

This notion of duality is also central to Robert Louis Stevenson's famous novella *Strange Case of Dr Jekyll and Mr Hyde* in which Hyde is the double of Jekyll and *vice versa*. The word "strange" in the title may even have inspired Maupassant to invent the name "horla". Stevenson's story was published a year prior to 'Le Horla' and Maupassant very probably knew about it. There are significant similarities between O'Brien's and Stevenson's stories.

When the strange event occurs in 'What Was It?', Harry Escott has been smoking opium:

> A strange perversity dominated the currents of our thought. They would not flow through the sun-lit channels into which we strove to divert them. For some unaccountable reason they constantly diverged into dark and lonesome beds, where a continual gloom brooded.[10]

Shortly before the invisible creature appears, the narrator therefore undergoes adverse reactions to opium, recalling Henry Jekyll's descriptions of the dramatic effect of his drug. In fact, smoking opium gives Escott a "boundless feeling of existence" comparable to the experience of Jekyll, who, by drinking his drug, acquires Hyde's energy, strength, and vitality. This "other" being might therefore be the corollary of the consumption of a drug, just as some commentators have interpreted Hyde. The invisible being would then be a drastically altered manifestation of the narrator: "God grant that I am not mad, and that this is not an insane fantasy!".[11] Is Harry Escott in a state of delerium? And creating the other being in a hallucinatory neurosis?

While Stevenson's and Dostoevsky's stories deal with the concept of the doppelgänger—"the apparition of a living person; a double, a wraith"[12]—there is no physical manifestation of the invisible being in 'What Was It?'. The first time the narrator mentions it, he explains that "[d]oors were opened without any visible agency."[13] "Agency", according to the OED, can refer to an "action or instrumentality *embodied* or *personified* as concrete existence (my emphasis)". This creature, therefore, has an existence, a corporeal form, but its body remains invisible to the naked eye. Since the narrator can apprehend the creature via all of his senses but sight, he decides to cast the creature in plaster with the help of a physician, thus revealing the creature's human shape. We may then wonder if this incorporeal *human-shaped* creature is a superior being.

In November 1859, Darwin published *On the Origin of Species*. This new theory must have been at the back of Maupassant's mind when he wrote:

> Nous sommes quelques-uns, si peu sur ce monde, depuis l'huître jusqu'à l'homme. Pourquoi pas un de plus, une fois accomplie la période qui sépare les apparitions successives de toutes les espèces diverses?[14]

'What Was It? A Mystery' was published only a few months *before* Darwin's revolutionary oeuvre. I make no claim that O'Brien was inspired by Darwin's works but he may have felt that this creature could embody a superior being, thus anticipating the soon-to-be groundbreaking discovery. In fact, this being may be capable of overpowering man: Escott engages in a "deadly" battle against this assailant which "looked as if it was capable of feeding on human flesh."[15] The survival of the narrator is therefore at stake and O'Brien skilfully builds suspense so that the reader fears for Escott's life. Will he meet the same tragic fate that later befell Dr Jekyll?—

> Will Hyde die upon the scaffold? or will he find courage to release himself at the last moment? God knows; I am careless; this is my true hour of death, and what is to follow concerns another than myself. Here then, as I lay down the pen and proceed to seal up my confession, I bring the life of that unhappy Henry Jekyll to an end.[16]

—or consider taking his own life as Maupassant's narrator later did in 'Le Horla'?

> Non…non…sans aucun doute, sans aucun doute…il n'est pas mort…Alors…alors…il va donc falloir que je me tue, moi!...[17]

However, O'Brien's narrator is eventually spared since the creature dies just before the end of the narrative. Nonetheless, the final lines suggest that Escott may have similarly disappeared:

> As I am on the eve of a long journey from which I may not return, I have drawn up this narrative of an event the most singular that has ever come to my knowledge.[18]

Since the creature dies at the end of the narrative when

Escott himself is taking leave of the story, one might wonder if the author's voice has not taken over in these final lines and if his presence does not in fact pervade the entire story. When Dr Hammond says that "he could write a story like Hoffman tonight, if [he] were only master of a literary style,"[19] the fact that this other horror story writer is mentioned draws our attention to the writer of the supernatural story we are reading. The authorial presence is further strengthened when Escott tells his fellow boarders that he has published a ghost story in *Harper's Monthly* where 'What Was It?' appeared.

With this in mind, we may therefore argue that there is more than meets the "I" in the line quoted above: "I have drawn up this narrative of an event." This may be an instance of authorial intrusion: the author of the short story is admitting the apocryphal nature of the story that has just been narrated. In fact, in the OED entry for "draw", we are reminded that this verb also signifies "to bring together by sewing; to mend; cf. also *draw up.*" There is thus a correlation between text and textile,[20] between the telling of a story and the creation of textile, which leads us to the phrase "to spin a yarn." In 'What Was It?', the creature is securely fastened with ropes and the garden displays "on washing-days rather too much clothes-*line*":[21] both the enigmatic creature and the haunted house are therefore *tied up* in this *literary yarn*. The image of the house enshrouded in a web could therefore symbolize the spinning of this apocryphal tale. When the narrator states at the very beginning "I have, I trust, the literary courage to face unbelief" O'Brien may be ironically referring to the fact that he is *the* "master of a literary style" who will use his storytelling skills to trick the reader and ensnare him or her in this supernatural tall tale. After all, "to draw" is also synonymous with "to lead, entice, allure" (OED).

When the "I" is directly implicated in a seemingly implausible story, it is all the more difficult to take the events at face value. Nonetheless, O'Brien is crafty and succeeds in casting doubt over the existence of an invisible creature. The latter might at times appear as a subconscious, antithetical, or schizophrenic manifestation of the narrator, or a harbinger of a new era where man's survival is at stake. The uncanny and proleptic references to the existence of a demonic "other" invite us to consider Fitz-James O'Brien both as a Tiresias figure anticipating later scientific research and as a forerunner of some of the greatest short stories of the second half of the 19th-century focusing on the complexities of the human mind.

Notes

1 For contemporary readers there was an additional mystery as the name of the writer did not accompany the story in the magazine in which it was published and many thought it was a piece of journalism rather than a fiction.

2 This is the pattern followed by works written after 'What Was It?' that also draw on the theme of invisibility and the supernatural.

3 My italics. Guy de Maupassant, *Le Horla*. Paris: Editions Gallimard, 1986, p.37.

4 *Ibid.*, p. 20. It is interesting to point out that Maupassant was born on August 5 (5/08) and the story of 'Le Horla' begins on May 8 (8/05). There is thus an interesting (deliberate?) inversion, which could suggest a link between the writer and the narrator of this story.

5 My italics. 'What was It? A Mystery', p.10.

6 My italics. William Shakespeare, *Richard III*. Oxford: Oxford University Press, 2000, p.343.

7 'What Was It? A Mystery', p.3.

8 Had Yeats's work been written prior to O'Brien's short story, it would have been very tempting to see a reference to *A Vision* in the following lines: "Black afreets continually arose from the depths of our talk [...] until they blotted every thing bright from our *vision*. Insensibly we yielded to the *occult* force that swayed us" (my italics). 'What Was It? A Mystery', p.8.

9 O'Brien couldn't have read the text himself, but a Russian-speaking acquaintance could have at least given him a summary of the story.

10 'What Was It? A Mystery', p.8.

11 *Ibid.*, p.16.

12 *The Oxford English Dictionary,* hereafter abbreviated to OED.

13 'What Was It? A Mystery', p.4.

14 Guy de Maupassant, *Op. Cit.*, p.73.

15 'What Was It? A Mystery', p.19.

16 Robert Louis Stevenson, *Strange Case of Dr Jekyll & Mr Hyde*. London: Penguin, p.97.

17 Guy de Maupassant, *Op. Cit.*, p.80.

18 'What Was It? A Mystery', p.20.

19 *Ibid.*

20 We may here refer to Roland Barthes's works or to the OED etymology of the word "text": "a. F. texte, also ONF. tixte, tiste (12th c. in Godef.), the Scriptures, etc., ad. med.L. textus the Gospel, written character (Du Cange), L. textus (u-stem) style, tissue of a literary work (Quintilian), lit. that which is woven, web, texture, f. text-, ppl. stem of tex-re to weave."

21 My emphasis. 'What Was It? A Mystery', p.10.

Not a Spook: A Personal Response to 'What Was It? A Mystery'

Dr Mathew D. Staunton

1. Introduction

I first read Fitz-James O'Brien's 'What Was It? A Mystery' when I was well into my thirties and living in Paris. Favourable comparisons with Poe and Stevenson, and the promise of an invisible monster had prepared me for a treat but I wasn't expecting the powerful emotional reaction that I eventually had to this strange little tale.

Ostensibly, this is the story of a pair of clueless American bachelors living in a Manhattan boarding house in the 1850s. After rebuffing a surprise attack by an invisible strangler, they tie it up and wring their hands for several weeks as it starves to death. The narrator, Harry Escott, claims that he has tried everything to keep his captive alive but not once does he consider releasing it or calling in outside help. Here is his description of the creature's death:

> Ten, twelve days, a fortnight passed, and it still lived. The pulsations of the heart, however, were daily growing fainter, and had now nearly ceased altogether. It was evident that the creature was dying for want of sustenance.

> While this terrible life struggle was going on, I felt miserable. I could not sleep of nights. Horrible as the creature was, it was pitiful to think of the pangs it was suffering.
>
> At last it died. Hammond and I found it cold and stiff one morning in the bed. The heart had ceased to beat, the lungs to inspire. We hastened to bury it in the garden. It was a strange funeral, the dropping of that viewless corpse into the damp hole.[1]

Crucially, there are no repercussions for either of the men because nobody cares about the fate of their victim. I use the word "victim" very deliberately here because without the intervention of Escott and his friend Hammond, the creature would not be dead at the end of the story. Essentially, then, this is a narrative of abuse: two middle-class, Anglo-Saxon men torture and kill a being that is smaller but otherwise not very different from themselves and get away with it scot-free because it is invisible. In one of the very first tales to feature an invisible character, invisibility is presented as a very definite curse.

What surprised me most about this tale was that it didn't evoke 19th century New York for me at all. Instead, I was transported back to 1980s Dublin, and memories of growing up on the Northside of the city were reactivated with a vengeance. I remembered one of my secondary school teachers reading interminable passages from *The Adventures of Huckleberry Finn*. I remembered my reaction to the death of a minor character in a British comic. I also remembered very clearly how I felt when a man was beaten to death in Fairview Park and his killers allowed to walk free. More than anything, though, I remembered the culture of abuse that permeated Irish society at the time and just how dangerous it was to be a child.

2. Les Invisibles de la rue d'Ulm

In 2009 I co-organized a conference and curated an exhibition in Paris to explore 'What Was It?' and its significance for 21st century readers.[2] Speakers and exhibitors used the tale as a vehicle to talk about social and historical invisibility, and made fruitful connections between O'Brien's invisible creature and the Armenian genocide,[3] the history of African-Americans,[4] and homelessness.[5] Collectively, we also told the story of Brice, a man who sleeps on front of the student cafeteria on Rue Erasme in the 5th arrondisement, very close to both the exhibition space at the Irish Cultural Centre and the conference venue at the Bibliothèque Sainte-Barbe.

Having lived on the street for many years, Brice has a very clear understanding of what it means to be invisible and the constant danger that this implies. As is the case in many Western nations, homeless people in France are perceived as lesser citizens or even non-citizens. Sociologist Laura Huey argues that this is only to be expected. "The notion that civil or human rights are inalienable is a piece of romantic Enlightenment fiction",[6] definitions of citizenship are increasingly exclusive, and rights "are directly linked to the exercise of civic responsibilities, foremost of which is to function as productive producers and consumers within the marketplace."[7] As lesser and non-citizens, these failed consumers do not benefit from the protection of the state to the same degree that their wealthier compatriots do and are the invisible victims of exploitation, violence, and a wide range of crimes.

Brice, however, has found a simple remedy: he sells books to passers-by. This gives him a recognizable and respectable purpose, and any money that changes hands is part of a satisfyingly commonplace commercial exchange. He is also visible to the police to the extent that he can use their coffee machine and toilet facilities whenever he wants. Those who sleep near him on the street also benefit from the visibility that this exchange generates and have become visible themselves. In conversation, Brice explained to me how that visibility is very welcome but not always helpful. Sometimes people call an ambulance while he is trying to sleep because they see him lying on the ground and fear the worst. The homeless people living nearby on Rue d'Ulm are not so easily seen and can lie down where they choose—in a telephone box on front of the Lebanese Church, on the ventilation grill across the road, on a traffic island, or at the end of the street in the shadow of the Pantheon, with its enormous dedication to the great men of France—without fear of interference from the general public.

3. Only a Nigger

During my first year in secondary school, my English teacher read large sections of *The Adventures of Huckleberry Finn* aloud in class, putting a lot of effort into creating distinct voices and accents for each character. It started out as a selection of entertaining (and sometimes pedagogically significant) passages but, after a few days, it drifted into an unabridged performance. It wasn't a complete waste of time, however. Far from it. As the weeks progressed, I discovered something in Mark Twain's vision of antebellum Southern society that chimed with my own developing understanding of the world. Along with the exotic concept of loaves of bread filled with mercury floating down the Mississippi, it was the reactions of the different characters to Jim, the escaped slave, and the treatment of black people in general that captured my attention. Dublin, it seemed to me, had its fair share of Jims and I understood that, just as in Twain's fiction, some lives were worth considerably less than others.

One passage has stayed in my head for almost thirty years. Towards the end of the book, Huckleberry Finn arrives at the house of Tom Sawyer's Aunt Sally and is mistaken for his friend. Put on the spot to explain why he is late, Huckleberry invents the sort of technical problem that riverboats were prone to at the time:

> "It warn't the grounding—that didn't keep us back but a little. We blowed out a cylinder-head."
>
> "Good gracious! anybody hurt?"
>
> "No'm. Killed a nigger."
>
> "Well, it's lucky; because sometimes people do get hurt. Two years ago last Christmas, your uncle Silas was coming up from Newrleans on the old Lally Rook, and she blowed out a cylinder-head and crippled a man. And I think he died afterwards. He was a Babtist."[8]

Arguably, this short exchange is the quintessence of the book as a whole. The notions that black people are nobodies and that their deaths are insignificant[9] are so commonplace in Southern society that Twain has Huckleberry embellish a lie with a dead "nigger". He could have left this detail out entirely and it might seem utterly pointless to invent an accidental death that elicits no reaction, but Huckleberry reads Aunt Sally well enough to know that this will fit perfectly with her worldview and make his story all the more believable. The contrast between the conventional emotional response to the account of an accidental death and the ephemeral, emotionless nature of its telling here makes these words resonate through the remainder of the book. The narrative of the death and burial of O'Brien's invisible creature has a similar force.

Twain was an outspoken supporter of abolition, emancipation, and civil rights, and regularly deconstructed and attacked the treatment of non-whites[10] in his writings and speeches. One famous example is particularly pertinent here. An anonymous editorial article attributed to Twain appeared in the Buffalo Express in 1869 in the wake of the lynching "by mistake" of a black man. Entitled 'Only a Nigger', it points a viciously sarcastic finger at a society in which it is the mistaken identity of a man rather than his brutal murder that is newsworthy:

> Ah, well! Too bad to be sure! A little blunder in the administration of justice by Southern mob-law, but nothing to speak of. Only "a nigger" killed by mistake — that is all.[11]

Again, the perceived worthlessness of the life of a black man and the invisibility that surrounds his existence and annihilation are thrown into sharp relief by the tone of the article. The man is excluded from the rights, protections, and rituals that his white neighbours enjoy in much the same way that the homeless people of Paris are excluded. He is not a part of their civilization and can be liquidated on a whim.

In both the *Buffalo Express* article and *Huckleberry Finn*, Twain exposes and tinkers with the mechanism that renders black people and their treatment invisible. Ralph Ellison eloquently describes this mechanism as

> ...a peculiar disposition of the eyes of those with whom [he] comes in contact. A matter of the construction of their inner eyes, those eyes with which they look through their physical eyes upon reality.[12]

This is no anatomical anomaly. Perception is not a natural attribute. It is a social activity, learned and cultivated. We perceive only what is deemed worthy of our attention and push all that is not into the background.[13] Huckleberry can mimic the reactions of the people around him but it is clear to the reader that he does not perceive the world as they do: his inner eye is more closely aligned with his physical eyes. He has suffered at the hands of his father and knows abuse when he sees it. He is also very close to being a non-citizen himself and inhabits a realm that borders that of the two dead "niggers". Twain invites us to recalibrate our inner eyes and be more like Huckleberry; to develop empathy, become critical thinkers, and magnify rather than gloss over the disturbing realities of American life.

4. The Wonder Gaze

Just after we had dismantled our exhibition in May 2009, I discovered a similar invitation to recalibrate the inner eye in the work of American artist Ken Gonzales-Day. Wallpapered across a corner of the 'Spy Numbers' exhibition[14] in the Palais de Tokyo was a large black and white photograph of a group of people clustered around a tree at night. It was mysterious and uncanny. Clearly, some sort of collective activity or ritual was underway but what were these people doing? It is only when I read the title card that the image revealed its sinister secret: it was a photograph of the aftermath of a lynching with the victim and the rope airbrushed out. Uncanny suddenly became shocking, chilling, horrifying in a spontaneous perceptual reversal.

'The Wonder Gaze (St. James Park)' (see pages 146-7) is an image from the 'Erased Lynching' series produced by Gonzales-Day between 2002 and 2011. It is very much a historiographical work. In the course of his research for a project on the omission of Latino subjects from Californian history,[15] Gonzales-Day discovered that there had been hundreds of such lynchings in the state. His artistic response was to reproduce the souvenir postcards and other photographic materials he had unearthed, carefully erasing all traces of the victim or victims from each image. This is how he explains this project on his website:

> The Erased Lynching series (2002-2011) sought to reveal that racially motivated lynching and vigilantism was a more widespread practice in the American West than was believed, and that in California, the majority of Lynchings were perpetrated against Latinos, Native

> Americans, and Asian Americans; and that more Latinos were lynched in California than were persons of any other race or ethnicity.
>
> The images derive from appropriated lynching postcards and archival materials in which the lynch victim and the ropes have all been been removed; a conceptual gesture intended to direct the viewers attention, not upon the lifeless body of the lynch victim, but upon the mechanisms of lynching themselves: the crowd, the spectacle, the photographer, and even consider the impact of flash photography upon this dismal past. The perpetrators, if present, remain fully visible, jeering, laughing, or pulling at the air in a deadly pantomime. As such, this series strives to make the invisible visible.[1]

He argues that the absences and empty spaces in these photographs are "emblematic of the forgotten history" of lynching in California.[17] This, however, has nothing to do with absent-mindedness. The minds of successive generations of historians, social commentators, politicians, educators, and citizens have deliberately absented themselves, refused to see these murders, denied their existence. The souvenir postcards were not used to remember but to remove the hanging bodies of Latinos, Asians, and Native Americans from the Californian imaginary. Reified and dehumanized, they became nobodies, like Twain's dead "nigger". Their violent deaths were nothing more than entertaining spectacles, stripped of meaning, and ultimately hidden. By removing them from these photographs, Gonzales-Day reinserts them into history and our consciousness. We have no choice but to see.

The Wonder Gaze (St. James Park)
Courtesy of Ken Gonzales-Day & Louis De Jesus Los Angeles

5. Nobody died today

While Twain's vision of the Deep South was slowly unfolding in the classroom, I was spending a considerable amount of my free time immersed in a very different kind of literature: the British science-fiction comic anthology *2000AD*. My local newsagent had instructions to set a copy aside for me each week and, whenever I had enough money, my Saturdays were dedicated to hunting for back issues in the Abbey Mall and the Alchemist's Head.[18] A regular winner of the 'Best Comic (Britain)' and 'Best Comic in the World awards',[19] *2000AD* has featured the writing talents of Alan Moore, Alan Grant, Pat Mills, John Wagner, Grant Morrison, and Neil Gaiman, and the artwork of Dave Gibbons, Carlos Ezquerra, Ian Gibson, Bryan Talbot, Brian Bolland, and Mike McMahon.

As a teenager I was a huge fan of the ultraviolent and utterly dystopian *Judge Dredd* and *Rogue Trooper* stories and followed them with a near-religious fanaticism. In the long term, though, it is the more subtle and poetic *Ballad of Halo Jones* by Alan Moore and Ian Gibson that I have repeatedly returned to. Serialized between 1984 and 1986, and still in print as a graphic novel today, this is the groundbreaking story of a 50th-century, working-class woman and her adventures on a floating residential ghetto and a luxury space liner, and as a soldier in a total interstellar war.

This story was "groundbreaking" because Halo was a well-written and unheroic female character in a universe dominated by male and macho *Übermenschen*. In the introduction to the 2013 reprint of *Halo Jones*, South African writer Lauren Beukes has this to say about the character she calls her "first role model":

> She's remarkable for being just a girl caught up in extraordinary circumstances. Halo is working class, she doesn't have any superpowers, in her own words, she was "just there".
>
> But she's being disingenuous. Because she got herself "there", driven by curiosity, dodging the cosy suck of conformity, straight out of the future ghetto of the Hoop where shopping really is an expedition of horrorshow proportions (...) onto a luxury space cruiser as a hostess and catapulted into the dark heart of a time-bending war of atrocity.
>
> Halo moves on, always on. She rolls with the gut punches, finds a way to get up again, wounded but not beaten, even as she loses everyone close to her. When he's not subverting the nature of what story is, Alan Moore is a perfect story teller. Not a word is wasted, events fold back on themselves. A rat dies and a war detonates. A nobody becomes somebody in a moment of terrible grace.[20]

Not surprisingly, it is the nobody who becomes somebody that I'm interested in here. Throughout Book II of *Halo Jones*, an anonymous, androgynous character wanders in and out of the action, unnoticed by all the people and animals (s)he encounters. When, for a brief moment, Halo and her friend Toy manage to see him/her, the Glyph (this is how the character is known to readers) explains that as the result of 48 sex changes (s)he cannot remember his/her original gender and has become invisible to everyone around him/her. (S)he can do as (s)he pleases and has no difficulty finding food or shelter but is always utterly alone.[21]

The Glyph's back story. *The Ballad of Halo Jones,* Book II, Prog 3

The notion that someone can be or become socially invisible and suffer isolation, abuse, and violence as a result was not new in 1985. As we have seen above, Twain was fully aware of this phenomenon in the middle of the 19th century. Knowledge of the Indian caste system and the existence of a shunned, "untouchable" caste has been widespread since the early years of British rule and was described in Mulik Raj Anand's 1935 novel *Untouchable*. Ralph Ellison's *Invisible Man* did the same for black people in the United States in 1952. The popular culture of the second half of the 20th century is full of invisible characters. Robert Silverberg's often reprinted 1963 short story 'To

See the Invisible Man' is an excellent example[22] and Joss Whedon, a prominent figure in contemporary popular culture, explores the subject in an episode of *Buffy the Vampire Slayer* entitled 'Out of Mind, Out of Sight', in which an awkward young girl who is socially invisible to her cool classmates gradually becomes physically invisible.[23]

What is exceptional about *Halo Jones*, and the story of the Glyph in particular, is that it explored gender roles during a period of entrenched conservatism across the British Isles. Topless "Page Three" glamour models were all the rage and Judge Pickles was a household name because of his outspoken opinions (regularly translated into controversial judgements) about the "provocative" clothing of female rape victims and his disrespectful treatment of women in general. Homosexuality was illegal in Ireland and the age of consent for homosexuals in the UK was still five years higher than for heterosexuals.

In this context, the Glyph was an anomaly. (S)he was a person without a clear gender in a strictly gendered society. Not perceived as a full citizen, (s)he became completely imperceptible. The fact that the 50th century we discover in *Halo Jones* was as gendered and conservative as the 1980s allowed Moore and Gibson to explore sexual politics in what appeared to be a time and a place remote from their own. As in all dystopian fictions, they were able to point fingers and ask difficult questions without openly attacking the society they lived in.

When the Glyph is accidentally killed in an explosion, Halo and Toy immediately forget him/her. The last word is given to Toy. Echoing Huckleberry Finn, she says "Nobody Died Today" while Ian Gibson's image shows the Glyph's hand sticking out from a pile of twisted, smoking metal (see below). I remember the anger I felt at this ending. To be "nobody" and die without being noticed was horrific. I knew little of the Holocaust and nothing of other genocides at the time. I had seen images of slavery, abuse, and discrimination on television. One source of imagery was the 1979 German/Canadian television series *Huckleberry Finn and his Friends* which was repeated several times throughout the 1980s. A tamer version of both *Tom Sawyer* and *Huckleberry Finn* it nonetheless made the status of Jim and other black people crystal clear. Thanks to my English teacher, I made the connection between the Glyph and the imaginary dead "nigger". I also connected this character's suffering and unnoticed death to the experiences of people in my city. As I have said above, a culture of abuse dominated every aspect of Irish life and Dublin had its own population of Glyphs and Jims.

The Glyph dies. *The Ballad of Halo Jones,* Book II, Prog 8

6. … almost a Taliban-esque society

Same-sex sexual activity was not decriminalized in Ireland until 1993 and throughout the 1980s homosexuals did not receive the full protection of the Irish State, which was very much a fundamentalist Catholic regime. In a recent newspaper interview, Gabriel Byrne described the Ireland of his youth as "almost Tailban-esque".[24] Some readers objected to the word "almost". That this was still the case when I was a child, is evidenced by the investigation into the stabbing to death of Charles Self, a homosexual television designer, on 20 January, 1982. Thirty detectives were tasked with catching his killer but very quickly it emerged that they were concentrating their efforts on fingerprinting, photographing, and compiling files on as many members of the gay community as they could locate, the vast majority of whom had nothing to do with the victim. The Irish Council of Civil Liberties and the *Irish Times* collected statements and affidavits from homosexual men reporting that investigators had repeatedly harassed, threatened, verbally abused, humiliated, and deliberately misled them. Members of the Garda Siochána, it seems, repeatedly came to the men's homes and workplaces to maximize embarrassment while needlessly interrogating them about their sexuality.[25]

The growing suspicion that gay men were not perceived as full citizens by the police was reinforced in April of the same year when the General Secretary of the Garda Representative Association (GRA) declared that social values were plunging in Ireland because homosexuals were demanding rights. He went on to link these demands to an increase in crime[26]. The police, it seemed, had decided to follow their religious convictions. Would they protect only those who did likewise?

Eight months after the murder of Self, a gang of young men and boys (two of them soldiers in the Irish Air Force) ambushed Declan Flynn in Fairview Park and beat him to death. As he lay dying they emptied his pockets and stole his watch. When they were arrested, they confessed to a spree of similar attacks. They had spent the summer cleaning up the park, a gay cruising area, and chasing out the "steamers", they said. With the moral support of their families and friends, and untroubled by the police, they had beaten up and robbed approximately twenty men by the time they killed Flynn.[27]

Because they admitted to having deliberately armed themselves with tree branches, lain in wait, and lured Flynn to the site of the ambush, all five of the gang members were charged with murder. The judge, Mr Justice Seán Gannon, however, had other ideas and directed the jury to consider this crime as manslaughter rather than murder. Their attacks on 20 other men, the robbery, and the premeditation were not to be taken into consideration. There was no doubt that they had beaten Flynn to death and they were duly found guilty of the lesser crime. At this point, the judge revealed a similar mindset to the leader of the GRA and suspended all of the sentences. Flynn's perceived outlaw status (the gang had their hearts in the right place but shouldn't have taken the law into their own hands) seems to have been sufficient to mitigate the punishment. With a laughable warning that they would have to serve their sentences "if they got into trouble again" Judge Gannon let them walk free. Predictably (what other lesson could he have taken away with him?), Robert Armstrong, the gang's ringleader, raped and robbed a pregnant woman in her home in 1992.[28]

The night of the sentencing revealed that the killing of homosexuals was a thing to be celebrated. Emboldened rather than humbled by their experience, the gang members led a victory march to the site of their crime, making it crystal clear that Declan Flynn's violent death was as much a lynching as that of Twain's "nigger" in 1869. The lack of protection for homosexuals and the lenient treatment of these vigilantes recalls the Southern justice that Twain railed against. Ken Gonzales-Day's 'Wonder Gaze' could be a snapshot of the post-trial celebrations in what is still one Dublin's of the most sinister parks

7. Children

O'Brien has his narrator describe the invisible creature as "small, not over four feet and some inches in height"[29] and weighing about the same as a fourteen-year old boy. For Kristine Hoyt Jouanne (see her essay in this volume) this detail is of the utmost importance. She convincingly links the diminutive size of the "Enigma" to the 1859 United States Supreme Court decision that confirmed and generalized the notion that slaves were property and the "Three Fifths Compromise" that counted them as a fraction of a human being for electoral purposes. I find this interpretation extremely attractive, chiming as it does with my reading of the tale in the light of *Huckleberry Finn*. Nonetheless, this is not the most compelling reading as far as I'm concerned. Things might be different were I reading the tale in *Harpers Magazine* in 1859. But as a 21st century reader at the mercy of my own experiences and culture, I cannot help but see this unfortunate creature as a child, and, more specifically, as an abused child.

Ireland, as I have suggested above, was a very dangerous

place for children in the 1980s. In the decades before independence children were weaponized by nationalists, who filled them with propaganda and groomed them for the coming revolution. After independence, the utility of these weapons evaporated and a culture of abuse quickly set in. The 1950s, 60s, and 70s were brutal times by any standard. The education system was fuelled by fear. Children were beaten with a wide range of home-made and purpose-made objects, threatened, humiliated, and psychologically abused by their teachers. There is plenty of oral evidence that teachers who did not use punishment straps and beat their pupils were bullied into doing so by their colleagues who wanted the culture of abuse to continue.[30] A concerted and systematic effort was made to train them like animals and they were conditioned by pain to obey. Parents lived in fear that any objection on their part would lead to their children receiving even more brutal treatment, being expelled, or being institutionalized. The police rarely investigated even the most severe abuse and judges were reluctant to convict even when they did. Public schools were bad enough but children and young people could also be locked up in even more abusive institutions like Industrial Schools and Magdalene Asylums on a whim.[31] And, of course, abuse was not restricted to the field of education. Children were not safe anywhere, and the home was a particularly risky environment. This was the case across the British isles. And still is. Graham Wilmer cites statistics put forward by Dr Nick Cooling, a leading psychiatrist specializing in sexual abuse trauma, in the account of his own traumatic experiences, *Conspiracy of Faith*:

> [I]f you took a typical street, anywhere in the country, you will find sexual abuse occurring in every fifth house, and one or more of the other forms of child abuse (neglect,

> emotional abuse and physical abuse) occurring in every third house, yet, child abuse is not talked about.[32]

The 'Sexual Abuse and Violence in Ireland' (SAVI) study conducted by the Health Services Research Centre in 2001 paints an even blacker picture.[33]

I grew up in slightly safer conditions than my parents and grandparents but abuse was, nonetheless, widespread, if not universal, and children were permanently at risk. By the time I started school, teachers could no longer use punishment straps, or beat children with sticks or with their hands, but they benefited from a contradictory and utterly surreal common law immunity from prosecution that lingered on until 1997.[34] Physical assaults on children by teachers were, therefore, commonplace. As a child I was slapped in the face, punched, had my hair and ears violently pulled, had my head banged against a door, and was made to stand with my arms outstretched and a bag in each hand for long periods. I was also repeatedly humiliated by certain teachers because of my name (not Gaelic enough), my address, the quality of my mother's car (a secondhand delivery van), and, incredibly, because I liked to read. Teachers were careful to leave no marks and the headmaster was an old hand at accusing pupils of exaggeration if they dared to tell their parents.

Physical and psychological abuse represented only the tip of a very ugly iceberg, however. In both my primary and secondary schools paedophiles operated openly and with the knowledge of the staff. One of my primary school teachers would pretend that boys were absent whenever the headmaster sent for them. No doubt, fearing for his job, he went no further than this small act of protection and defiance, and did not inform parents, officials, or the authorities that he suspected his colleague was abusing his pupils. In my secondary school, which was run by the Christian Brothers, one of my Irish teachers regularly wrestled with the boys during class and would often send pupils to another building to fetch a blue rubber mat from the gymnasium. His activities were known to the staff and the headmaster (boys carrying mats had to pass the staff room and the headmaster's office) but they chose to do nothing. This teacher was even allowed to organize theatre rehearsals in an empty building after school. One of his colleagues resigned in protest but chose not to inform parents or authorities of what he knew. And then, one day, after consistently turning a blind eye and deliberately compromising the safety of hundreds of boys, the headmaster was eventually faced with a complaint from parents that he couldn't deflect. His first impulse (fearing for his job, no doubt) was to call the Christian Brothers to ask for guidance rather than to contact the police. He discovered that the teacher was already under investigation for child abuse in another school. With the complicity of the police (no investigation was carried out in my school), the Christian Brothers, the headmaster, and the staff, my Irish teacher discreetly disappeared, went to jail, and was never mentioned again. Parents were never informed and the school's reputation was protected.

Outside school, things were equally dangerous. Abuse was rampant in sport. Standing alone at a bus stop would attract predators in cars. I was followed by people on my way to and from school. I was cornered by a policeman in uniform (most likely from Coolock Garda Station) while walking my dog and asked to guess what he had in his pocket. I was handcuffed by a security guard while playing on waste ground with a friend. Trusting adults simply wasn't an option.

I know few Irishmen of my generation who do not have a similar story to tell. Many stories are much worse. They are often so similar that we can tell them without resorting to language. Nods and exchanged looks are more than sufficient when everyone at the table has been through the same ordeal, and yet much of what has happened to children was and has remained invisible. The cases of the BBC in the UK and the Catholic Church everywhere have shown that sexual abuse can be successfully hidden when the protection of the institution comes first and adults are afraid for whatever reason to denounce colleagues or prominent figures. When you add the inadequacy or non-existence of complaints procedures, the historical incompetence of police forces and their unquestioning defence of people in positions of power, the fact that children are generally abused behind closed doors, in the family home, in a dressing room, and in headmasters' offices, the overwhelming difficulties faced by sufferers of PTSD in relationships, in interviews, and in courtrooms, it is not difficult to understand how abuse can be concealed. It must also be noted that those who abuse children generally go to great pains to create the impression that their behaviour is normal, and that the victim or the anxious colleague is the anomaly, not the perpetrator himself.

Data on how abuse is kept invisible in practice are, understandably, hard to come by. The sort of documentary evidence that historians tend to look for is extremely rare in this context. The 'Ferriter Report' (annexed to the 2009 'Ryan Report')[35] clearly demonstrates the futility of looking for evidence of abuse in the archives. The abusers of children do not write up their crimes. And those tasked with protecting them in Ireland have proved suspiciously careless with their files. The recent media interest in the long history of sexual abuse at the elite Caldicott School in Buckinghamshire, therefore, sheds much needed light on this very dark subject. The mechanisms used to hide abuse in this case can be fruitfully mapped onto the Irish system.

Testimony of former Caldicott pupils shows that the culture of the school made it next to impossible for children to speak out about their experiences:

> [I]f a teacher woke you in your dormitory bed late at night and called you into his room, you obeyed. When he pulled back his bed sheets, you climbed in. If he performed a sex act on you, simulated sex or penetrated you, you did not complain. And you most certainly knew not to tell anyone.[36]
>
> [...] Because of the age you are, you don't question anything. I had no reference in terms of an adult doing that sort of thing to me but I remember wanting to be in his favour."[37]

Investigations by police and journalists, and victim statements have revealed the "vice-like grip" of the headmaster on the school, its staff, and its pupils, and to what extent this allowed him and group of paedophile teachers to abuse boys for decades. When two teachers were exposed in the 1960s and 70s, their crimes were "hushed up, with tacit assistance from the education authorities". One teacher was questioned by education officials but police were not informed and he was never prosecuted. The second was banned from teaching for five years but never prosecuted after being ordered by the headmaster to lie his way out of his predicament: "…I don't care how you do it; you will have to deny your previous statement and tell lies if necessary. I am not having the school involved".[38] Both cases were quietly forgotten. I was struck by the similarity between these outcomes and the clandestine discussions that took place in my own school. The failure of the justice system to protect children was also very familiar. When the headmaster was finally charged with a string of sexual offences in 2003, the judge terminated the prosecution, "primarily on the basis that a trial would not be fair because [his] alleged offences were historical".[39]

There is no doubt that the invisibility of child abuse suits the adult establishment. Real investigation (the sort of zealous investigation that takes place in cases of copyright infringement today, for example) would lead to mass arrests, the closure of schools, the fall of governments, and would totally discredit entire police forces, justice systems, churches, and even states. Opening our (inner) eyes to what is happening to our youngest citizens as we try to convince them that they are living the best years of their lives (rather than satisfying ourselves with being suitably shocked at the handful of spectacular abuse cases exposed by the media) means staring at the very worst aspects of our civilization and ourselves.

8. Conclusion: Habeas Corpus?

In the 150 years since 'What was It? A Mystery' was published, the tale has lost none of its power to disturb. On the contrary, successive generations of readers have made fresh connections between the disenfranchised, abused, ignored, and discriminated against of their particular time and place, and the invisible, voiceless, and ultimately powerless thing that O'Brien's narrator and his friend starve to death in their home. The doctor's oath to protect his patients from harm, mischief, and injustice clearly does not apply in cases where the patient's body reflects no light and he/she has no family, community, or legal representation to defend him/her. And so it is in the real world, when we pass beyond the limits of the text, in states which have to be goaded by the United Nations to refrain from abusing their minorities and in republics which fail miserably to protect their weakest citizens as they actively persecute those of their neighbours.

It doesn't take a master criminal to get away with murder when the victim is nowhere to be seen.

Notes

1 'What Was It?', p.20.

2 The conference was called 'Obituaries of the Invisible' and took place on 15 May in the Bibliothèque Sainte-Barbe in Paris. It brought together design students from my school and researchers from Paris 3—Sorbonne Nouvelle. The exhibition was held at the Centre Culturel Irlandais from 14-19 May and was called 'A Rough Fac-simile of the Mystery'.'

3 Artist and illustrator Laure Fissore created a printed and blind embossed paper sculpture to explore the Great Crime of 1915.

4 Dr Kristine Hoyt Jouanne (see her contribution to this volume) read a provocative paper on the historical legal status of black people in the United States.

5 Steven Briand and Smail Kanouté showed a short film about the homeless people living in the neighbourhood.

6 Laura Huey, *Invisible Victims: Homelessness and the Growing Security Gap*. Toronto: University of Toronto Press, 2012, p.16.

7 *Ibid.*, p.15.

8 Mark Twain, *The Adventures of Huckleberry Finn*. New York: Harper & Bros., 1912, pp. 306-7.

9 It is important to note that the death of a slave would have been of the utmost importance to his/her owner because of the financial investment involved.

10 Twain also commented on the treatment of Chinese immigrants.

11 *Buffalo Express*, August 26, 1869

12 Ralph Ellison, *Invisible Man*. New York: Vintage, 1952, p.3.

13 Guillaume le Blanc explores this idea in detail in his *L'Invisibilité Sociale*. Paris: Presses Universitaires de France, 2009.

14 'Spy Numbers' took as its starting point the enigmatic broadcasts of Numbers Stations. These shortwave radio stations have been broadcasting sequences of numbers for decades but their function remains a mystery. It was this mystery and the disturbing sense of unseen and unfathomable conspiracy that it engenders that was explored by the exhibition.

15 Anna Meliksetian, 'California Strange Fruit: Ken Gonzales-Day's "Lynching in the West"'. http://www.kengonzalesday.com/press/essays/annameliksetian.htm. Retrieved 16 November 2013.

16 Retrieved from http://www.kengonzalesday.com/projects/erasedlynching/index.htm, the "Erased Lynching" page on the website of Ken Gonzales-Day, on 16 November 2013.

17 See ken Gonzales-Day, *Lynching in the West, 1850-1935.* Durham: Duke University Press, 2006, and http://www.kengonzalesday.com

Notes

18 In the days before the Celtic Tiger, the Abbey Mall was a haven for alternative record shops and comic dealers. The Twilight Zone was the shop we bought our comics in. The Alchemist's Head, as its name suggests, was an occult shop in essex Street that also sold new and second-hand comics.

19 Archives of the National Comic Awards: http://www.hahnlibrary.net/comics/awards/national.php. Retrieved 4 October, 2013.

20 Lauren Beukes in Alan Moore and Ian Gibson, *The Ballad of Halo Jones*. Oxford: Rebellion, 2013, introduction, [n.p.].

21 *Ibid.*, Prog 8.

22 A man is sentenced to a year of invisibility as punishment for his antisocial behaviour. The people he meets can still see him, but they are required by law to act as if they cannot. He enjoys himself at first, going to the cinema for free and walking into women's locker rooms but when he gets sick, no one will treat him and he becomes increasingly depressed. The story was adapted for television in 1985 and aired as episode 16b of *The New Twilight Zone*

23 *Buffy the Vampire Slayer*, season 1, episode 11. Story by Joss Whedon, Teleplay by Ashley Gable and Thomas A. Swyden

24 *Sunday Independent*, 22 September, 2013

25 *Irish Times*, Monday, 22 March, 1982, p.6; Wednesday, March 31, 1982, p.4.

26 *Irish Times*, Monday, April 5, 1982, p.13.

27 *Irish Times*, Wednesday, 9 March, 1983, p.9.

28 *Irish Independent*, 20 June, 2013.

29 'What Was It? A Mystery', p.19.

30 Three sources, all teaching in secondary schools before and after corporal punishment was officially in use, confirmed that they were bullied into using punishment straps by older colleagues. One was even driven to the shop which sold the straps in the city centre and forced to buy one.

31 This is demonstrated by the research carried out by the School-children's Protection Organisation in the 1950s. Their pamphlet *Punishment in Our Schools* makes chilling reading and includes letters from distraught parents expressing their fears for their childrens' safety in a system that guaranteed abuse, protected the abusers, and punished anyone who complained about it. Dublin: The Organisation, 1955.

32 Quoted in Graham Wilmer, *Conspiracy of Faith: Fighting for Justice after Child Abuse.* Cambridge: The Lutterworth Press, 2007, p.126.

33 H. McGee, R. Garavan, M. de Barra, J. Byrne, & R. Conroy, *The SAVI Report: Sexual Abuse and Violence in Ireland*. Dublin: The Liffey Press, 2002.

Notes

34 In 1982, Education Department Circulars 9/82 and 5/82 stated that corporal punishment should no longer be used, but teachers' immunity from criminal prosecution was only removed by article 24 of the Offences Against the Person (Non Fatal) Act 1997, which states: "The rule of law under which teachers are immune from criminal liability in respect of physical chastisement of pupils is hereby abolished."

35 The Commission to Inquire into Child Abuse was established in 2000 "with functions including the investigation of abuse of children in institutions in the State". Its final report, better known as the 'Ryan Report', was published in May 2009. The 'Ferriter Report' is inlcuded in volume five of this document as an appendix. This latter report was submitted by Dr (now Prof) Diarmaid Ferriter in June 2006 in an attempt to provide historical insights into child abuse in Ireland. This attempt was, in my opinion, a miserable failure, but serves, nonetheless, to highlight the methodological and ethical issues inherent in archival research when the archives are maintained and manipulated by the perpetrators of crimes against children and those who benefit from hiding those crimes. A blurred copy of the 'Ferriter Report' has been available for several years on the Commission's website: http://www.childabusecommission.ie/rpt/05-05.php. A request to the webmaster to upload a readable copy has, to date, been fruitless. It can also be found in the hardcopy and digital versions of the *Report of The Commission to Inquire into Child Abuse*. Dublin: Government Publications, 2009.

36 Andrew Norfolk in *The Times*, Wednesday, 18 December, 2013, p.6.

37 *Ibid.*, p.7

38 *Ibid.*, p.6.

39 *Ibid.*, p.7.

About the Authors

Agnès Fourtané: An English teacher, she has taught students both in economics and management, and secondary school pupils in France. She has been interested in Irish studies and translation for many years. She lived in Ireland for over a year and has spent time there on a regular basis. As part of her Masters degree in Irish Studies, she did research on Irish perceptions of Australia and on family emigration from Ireland. She also translated 'Homesickness', a short story by George Moore. She then did research on the French translations of John Millington Synge's dramatic works. She has also translated various texts in the fields of documentaries (Doc Net Films) and academic research (CNRS, Obedience.net ...).

Feargus Gwynplaine MacIntyre was a wonderful storyteller, journalist, novelist, poet, and illustrator. His best known works are the science-fiction novel *The Woman Between the Worlds* and the anthology of verse and humour *MacIntyre's Improbable Bestiary*. His stortelling extended to his own childhood and biography so we don't know anything for sure about who he really was but we have no reason not to believe that he was born in Scotland, lost his parents at an early age, and somehow ended up in an Australian orphanage. He lived for much of his adult life in New York and worked nights as a printer to free up his days for research and writing. He took his own life on June 25, 2010.

Kristine Hoyt Jouanne. After completing her PhD studies in French literature with an emphasis on the 19th century and the novelist Emile Zola—her thesis dealt with Food and Eating imagery and symbolism in Zola's series of novels known as the "Rougon-Macquart"—at the University of Iowa, Kristine relocated to Paris where she lives with her daughter and works as a Professor of English at top-rated SKEMA Business School, France's leading political institute, Sciences-po, and ENSAD, one of the country's premier schools of design and applied arts. She is also a translator and business English coach.

Rethabile Masilo is a Mosotho poet who enjoys reading and writing. He lives in Paris with his wife and two children. Rethabile is self-employed and works in language-teaching. He says he has been writing for a good while, learning through trial and error and picking up lots of sounds by reading and re-reading the poems that he likes. His work has been published in various magazines and online.

Born in 1961 in Lesotho, he left his country with his parents and siblings to go into exile in 1980. He moved through the Republic of South Africa (a very short stay, on account of the weight of Apartheid), Kenya, and The United States of America, before settling in France in 1987.

He blogs at *Poéfrika* and co-edits with Phil Rice the literary magazine *Canopic Jar*.

Cécile Chartier is currently completing her PhD on Fitz-James O'Brien under the supervision of Professor Bonafous-Murat at Université Paris 3 Sorbonne-Nouvelle. She previously worked on the Gothic and fantastic veins in novels and short stories (Sheridan Le Fanu, Bram Stoker, Lafcadio Hearn...) She now teaches English-language literature, translation and media studies at Université d'Evry-Val d'Essonne.

Alexandra Tauvry is a fourth-year PhD student in the School of English in Trinity College Dublin. She is an Irish Research Council Postgraduate Scholar and is part of the 'Texts, Contexts, Cultures' PhD programme. Her thesis focuses on Northern Irish writer Paul Muldoon and the themes of autobiography and autofiction.

Mathew D Staunton: Originally from Coolock in Dublin, Mathew is a historian, teacher, and printmaker. He divides his time between having fun with his daughter, Aoife, research, teaching, making books, and printing on a small press at the bottom of his garden. He also edits and illustrates for Everytpe in Mayo and runs The Onslaught Press in Oxford.

www.ingramcontent.com/pod-product-compliance
Lightning Source LLC
Chambersburg PA
CBHW022209050726
47590CB00002B/716

9780992723804